The
Monetary Muddle

The
Monetary Muddle

Compilation and Commentary by
Thomas G. Evans

INTRODUCTION

A mere four years ago, the question, "How's the dollar been doing lately?," would have received puzzled looks and little or no response from a group of business students or financial executives. Back in 1970, international monetary affairs was not a commonly popular topic and received little coverage in the financial and regular media. Instead, this topic was considered the special interest of a select group of international experts.

How different are things today! Now that same question would be perfectly natural and should receive the appropriate response from the groups cited. For today, almost daily, we find the events and developments in the world monetary markets reported by both the financial and regular press and thereby brought to our attention. Indeed, in light of the amount of coverage given these topics today, one must conclude that the world monetary system is one of the most prominent issues of 1973-74!

What has caused this change? The primary reason is that within this recent period there have been two major crises in the world monetary system, resulting in two historic devaluations of the American dollar and the floating of many other major currencies. In addition, recent growths in international trade and investment and recent political and economic events relating to the Middle East and the world energy crisis have focused the world's attention on international economic interdependence and the world monetary system, which makes up much of the environment for international business and investment.

The natural result of this interest and attention is that a great deal of interest in these topics has arisen in colleges, universities, and business firms. This in turn has created the need for a book to provide a concise, easily understood, and relevant selection of recent articles on the topics related to international monetary affairs and the recent world monetary crises. This book needs two characteristics to meet the needs of today:

1. It must be current, timely, and up to date so as to include the most recent developments in the world monetary system. This is extremely important in light of the dynamic character of international monetary affairs.

2. It must include both basics and current complex issues. Wherever possible, background information should be included for those with little previous exposure to international monetary affairs to facilitate an understanding of the contemporary issues. In addition, the whole presentation should be written in a practical business style to aid in this understanding.

This book of recent articles from *The Wall Street Journal* is a response to these factors. It is designed to provide a current selection of articles on the 1973 world monetary crisis and related issues in international monetary affairs. The articles were selected from *The Wall Street Journal* for their timeliness, readability, and practical orientation. It is primarily intended for use at both the undergraduate and graduate levels in any college or university course concerning international trade, business, or monetary affairs as a current supplement to the text. It can also be used as a major source in seminars or courses in such specialized areas of international business as international accounting, finance, and multinational corporate operations. It is also appropriate for financial executives who desire to refresh or update their understanding of world monetary affairs. It was with these goals in mind that this text was compiled.

—THOMAS G. EVANS

Dayton, Ohio

Contents

Contents

Contents

Part I

Major Developments in the 1973 World Monetary Crisis

BACKGROUND

The international monetary system has been one of the most dynamic and volatile areas of international business in recent years and has undergone tremendous change. It is also a very important area, since the world monetary system helps form the environment for international trade and investment and all three areas are highly interrelated.

Part I of this text traces chronologically the major events and developments that were a part of the 1973 world monetary crisis. To place these developments into their proper context, two previous events must be considered first:

1. After World War II, in 1944, the major non-Communist nations of the world formed the International Monetary Fund in an attempt to establish a flexible but stable system of exchange rates to promote international trade. The agreement among these nations (called the Bretton Woods Agreement) called for the United States to establish an official exchange rate for the dollar in terms of gold and for the other nations to establish official exchange rates for their currencies in terms of the dollar. All nations agreed to keep the actual market rate of exchange for their currencies within a band of 1% up or down from the official rate by either buying their currency with dollars or gold to increase its actual market rate or selling their currency for gold

or dollars to lower the market rate. In addition, any nation could alter its official rate through consultation with the IMF. If the new official rate was lower than the previous rate, this was called a devaluation; if higher, a revaluation. This arrangement continued through the nineteen-sixties, with periodic devaluations and revaluations. But during the nineteen-sixties, and especially the late sixties, the United States experienced a continual, large net outflow of dollars due to a number of factors. Although the dollar surplus nations were encouraged to revalue their currencies to help remedy the situation, many of them preferred to exchange their surplus dollars for American gold, which created a gold drain for the United States.

2. Thus, in August 1971, the United States suspended the link between the dollar and gold and refused to exchange gold for dollars. Over the next few months, other nations allowed their currencies to revalue in terms of the dollar and in December 1971, the IMF nations agreed to a new system of official exchange rates reflecting a lower value for the dollar (this was the first modern devaluation of the dollar). This new agreement (called the Smithsonian Agreement) allowed the actual market rates of exchange to fluctuate with a band of 2.25% up or down from the new official rates.

These two previous events provide the background needed to consider the monetary crisis which developed in 1973.

Commentary: Readings 1-10
The Crisis Emerges and Is Settled

The year 1973 began with the international monetary system beginning to totter. The Smithsonian Agreement, reached back in December 1971, was not working well and was in trouble. Speculation, uneven trade and payment balances resulted in continual intervention drains for certain currencies, especially the United States dollar. The strains grew until in early February, a new world monetary crisis again developed. As a result of this particular crisis, a new era in world monetary affairs would begin by the abandonment of the fixed rate monetary system associated with the Smithsonian and Bretton Woods agreements and the substitution of a new system of floating exchange rates. Largely as a result of the February 1973 crisis and the attempts to find a new monetary system that would work well in the long run, the floating system emerged as a temporary settlement until a new, more permanent solution to the chronic problems of the world's monetary system could be developed.

The events and developments of this period are covered by Readings 1-10. The crisis and its settlement happened quite rapidly, with the crisis emerging in early February and being settled by early March. The first five articles focus on the crisis and its immediate resolution. The first reading gives a sense of the urgency and suddenness of the crisis as it appeared in early February and presents some of its causes and underlying reasons. Reading 2 focuses on one immediate major outcome of the crisis: the second devaluation of the American dollar. Throughout this period, much negotiation and discussion took place among the world monetary leaders to settle the turmoil and effect a solution to the problems and many proposals and counter-proposals and suggestions were considered. This search for a solution is traced in Readings 2, 3 and 4.

Finally, in Reading 5, the world monetary system is seen to stabilize into a system of floating rates, linked floating rates (called a "joint float" or "snake"), and semi-floating rates (where some government intervention is present, called a "dirty float"). These five articles report on the events up to March 1973 and show how quickly, as a result of crisis, the world's monetary system changed from one with fixed rates, formality and certainty to one with floating rates, little uniformity and a great deal of uncertainty about the future status of this system. Most greeted the new system as an interim measure, with the anticipation that a better system could be negotiated later by the world monetary leaders.

During the next few months, the floating rate system had an opportunity to settle down and operate and be appraised. Articles and reports from this period are presented in Readings 6-8, which mainly deal with the major post-crisis developments and the continued search for a better world monetary system to replace the floating system. Reading 7 is especially important in that it brings into the scene a re-emerging factor which took some of the pressure off the new floating system only to make the world monetary situation more complex and confused: gold.* Reading 8 is a benchmark article which reviews the operations of the floating system for its first three months and evaluates its operations and effects. As shown in this article, the initial skepticism with which the floating system was greeted began to diminish as the system operated. But the negotiations and search for a better system continued.

* Reading 22, in Part II, may be read after 7 for more information on the reemergence of gold.

The efforts toward continued progress in negotiations toward a "long term" solution to the world's monetary problems is the theme of Readings 9-10. As the world monetary leaders began to look forward to the formal meeting of the International Monetary Fund in Nairobi in September, more evaluations of the floating system and suggestions for changes and predictions came forth. Although the floating system seemed to be working better and better and nations became better adjusted to it, there was still much anticipation that the Nairobi meetings would produce yet another change in the structure of the world monetary system.

Thus, in Readings 1-10, we are given insight into the emergence of the 1973 world monetary crisis, its settlement through the use of a new system of floating exchange rates of varying kinds, and the expectations that yet a second major change in the world monetary system would occur in 1973, at the fall meetings of the IMF in Nairobi.

On Your Mark

THE world monetary agreement is in tatters this morning, Feb. 12, 1973. Foreign-exchange markets in Tokyo, Paris and London are closed by order of their governments, and the German markets aren't likely to open either. Some important currencies may soon be changed in value or set afloat—allowed to drift freely beyond the values established when the last crisis hit a year or so ago. The dollar, meanwhile, is sinking like something that has been torpedoed—which indeed it has been.

There is, in short, yet another world monetary crisis. But, oddly, it's a crisis caused more by fear than by fundamentals. And, again oddly, it's a crisis that is actually good for America and its dollar.

Also, it's a crisis that again points up a hard reality: The world monetary system has no firm foundation. Despite efforts to find a substitute, the system is still based on the dollar, and when the dollar weakens (which has become a regular thing), the system collapses.

The latest crisis has been caused by a run on the dollar, primarily in West Germany but also in Japan, the Scandinavian nations and some other countries. The West German central bank had to buy $6 billion of dollars so far this month as speculators switched from weak dollars to strong marks. The run on the dollar apparently was triggered by the continuing U.S. deficit in world trade and the fears of a return to an unacceptable rate of inflation in the U.S.

The strengths and weaknesses of currencies are really based on supply and demand for them. Thus, a trade deficit weakens the dollar because it builds up a supply of that currency abroad—U.S. importers pay for their purchases in dollars—while there is no equal demand for the dollar from foreigners because they aren't buying many U.S. products. A fear of inflation weakens the dollar because inflation makes U.S. goods more expensive relative to foreign-made goods and thus less competitive in world markets; and the less competitive a nation is, the worse its trade deficit is likely to be.

Under an agreement reached at a meeting of world monetary men at the Smithsonian Institution in December 1971, various currencies were assigned new values in relation to one another—the dollar at the time was devalued, and the German mark and the Japanese yen were upvalued. It was figured that the new values more accurately reflected the relative international strengths of the nations. The men from the various nations then agreed to support the currencies at the new levels.

For instance, if supply and demand were in balance, it was figured, the dollar should be worth no less than 3.15 German marks. If the supply of dollars should exceed the demand at that price, the German central bank would buy all the excess dollars offered so that the parity would remain at 3.15. And that's what's happening now. But Germany has to pay for all those dollars with something, so it has to print more marks to pay the people who are turning in the dollars. And with more marks in their hands, Germans are willing to bid up the prices of goods and services—which causes worrisome inflation, which in turn is why central banks can't go on forever buying excess dollars and why the supply and demand must eventually be restored to a balance.

All the time the latest crisis has been abuilding, the West Germans have been insisting that they will continue to buy up dollars as they promised in the Smithsonian agreement. They won't let the mark float to higher levels, they have said, nor will they install a so-called two-tier system, as France, Italy and Belgium have done. (Under such a system, currencies used in commercial transactions are controlled at the Smithsonian rates, but currencies used in financial transactions, including speculations, are allowed to float to levels supported by supply and demand.)

But West Germany now has erected some barriers to the dollar inflows. It has restricted the borrowing of dollars, for instance, because borrowed dollars have been fueling the speculation. Still, the attack on the dollar has continued, and the thinking in other European lands is that Bonn will simply have to upvalue the mark pretty quickly. Bonn officials have continued to rule out such a politically unpopular move, which would weaken Germany competitively by making its exports more expensive in world markets.

The problem involves much more than the German mark alone or even the dollar alone. If the German mark is floated or revalued upward—some analysts predict a 10% rise—the Dutch guilder seems certain to follow, and the Swiss franc, already floating, probably also would be repegged at a higher rate. This is because of close economic ties among these countries. And the Japanese yen would also be affected making an upward revaluation of that strong currency more palatable to the Japanese exporters who compete with Germany in world markets.

Speculation on such moves raged in the world's capitals over this mid-February 1973 weekend, fueled by meetings of international financial officials.

In Paris, Paul Volcker, U.S. Treasury Under Secretary for Monetary Affairs, met with France's finance minister, Valery Giscard d'Estaing. The two-hour session, which followed meetings by Mr. Volcker with finance officials in Tokyo, Bonn and London, didn't produce any public comment on the talks.

Earlier, the French finance minister held a surprise meeting with Anthony Barber, Great Britain's chancellor of the exchequer, and Helmut Schmidt, a top West German financial official. A Japanese government official, Takashi Hosoomi, is scheduled to meet in Bonn with Mr. Schmidt. William Eberle, President Nixon's trade ambassador, was reported to have left Tokyo for Washington after warning the Japanese of possible unilateral U.S. actions such as an import surcharge, unless Tokyo helps American goods get free access to Japanese markets, the Associated Press reported.

In Basel, Switzerland, where central bankers from major nations were holding their regular monthly meeting with the Bank for International Settlements, discussions on easing the crisis continued. It was understood that one proposal concerned a possible widening of currency bands to 4.5% on each side of the central rate; at present, the price of the currency is allowed to fluctuate only 2.25% either way.

But central-bank governors can only suggest in a situation like this. It takes political decisions at a higher level to put those suggestions to work.

If the outcome of the crisis is unclear, its genesis is even murkier. "It really snuck up on us," says an international economist at a New York bank. "There's no reason for it, except that most foreign-exchange dealers are manic-depressive by nature."

On the economic fundamentals, despite the U.S. balance-of-payments deficits, the U.S. dollar should be relatively strong compared with other currencies, with the exception of the yen. That's because inflationary pressures in Europe are significantly stronger than in the U.S. and the productivity of the American economy is growing fast.

The figures on 12-month changes in inflation, for instance, show the U.S. rate at 3.4%. By comparison, the rates were 6.4% in Germany, 6.9% in France, 7.3% in Italy, 7.6% in England and 8.1% in the Netherlands. Another key figure, change in industrial output over 12 months, shows the U.S. up 10.4%, compared with 3.8% in Germany, 6.4% in France, 4.9% in Italy, 6.3% in England and 6.8% in the Netherlands. Similarly, real growth of the economy in the United States is far outpacing real growth in every major European nation.

Still, the announcement in January that Phase 2 had given way to Phase 3 in the U.S. was widely interpreted—or misinterpreted—in America and abroad as a removal of all wage and price controls and a signal that the rate of inflation would jump. Whether this will happen remains to be seen (the administration asserts it won't happen), but at any rate people who speculate and people who panic decided to unload their dollars.

"There is no crisis, except the one created by idiots on all sides," says Charles Stahl, editor of an economic newsletter in New York.

In the meantime, the U.S. is deriving some clear benefits from the monetary turmoil. "In weakness there is strength," one London-based American official says with a smile.

The more the mark and the yen are buffeted upward, the more competitive dollar-priced goods become in world markets. Although some analysts question the impact of exchange-rate changes on imports and exports, a weak dollar is bound to have some effect on increasing U.S. exports and decreasing its imports, thus in the long run helping the nation's balance of payments.

More immediately, the turmoil is reducing the upward pressure on a key element in the U.S. economy, short-term interest rates. As foreign central banks acquire dollars through their market intervention, they ask the New York Federal Reserve Bank to purchase U.S. government securities for their accounts, thus gaining some yield on their reserve assets. Such purchases, amounting to $1.66 billion in one recent week, help finance the U.S. budget deficit and reduce borrowing costs in the U.S. market, at least temporarily.

U.S. sources say privately the U.S. may be able to gain through disorderly forces of speculation the trade advantages that it didn't fully gain in the Smithsonian Agreement of 1971. "The U.S. would have accepted a bigger dollar devaluation then" than the roughly 8% agreed to, one expert says. Foreign governments simply wouldn't go along with anything greater at that time for fear of losing markets to the U.S. goods.

American officials are on record as having offered to devalue by as much as 10% prior to the Smithsonian meeting, and it's understood that they would have been just as happy with 12%, perhaps happier. While Washington has discretely avoided actions that would fan the speculation of further devaluation, in the past few weeks the Nixon administration clearly hasn't gone out of its way to dampen the speculation, either.

The main opportunity for the U.S. presented by the current turbulence is that Japan will overcome its reluctance to revalue the yen still further upward and thus diminish the flood of Japanese products into U.S. markets. The American authorities would like to see the German mark floated or upvalued because this would not only give direct help to U.S. businesses but would also make it politically easier for the Japanese to bow to U.S. pressure on the yen.

But, along with the benefits for the U.S., analysts on both sides of the Atlantic see severe and continuing problems for everyone in the monetary crisis. Most notably, they fear that exchange barriers erected in emergencies will be slow to come down when the crises are past. The only "plus" in this area is the hope that the current crisis will spur more urgent efforts to make fundamental reforms in the world's monetary system and trade relations among nations.

The danger in this crisis is that instead of producing currency revaluations that permit dismantling of present controls, it will panic governments into an ever-tighter and more protectionist network of restrictions on movement of money and goods. Such moves would harm the U.S. economy less than any other, but some diplomats worry that the weakening effect in Europe and Japan would strain the Western alliance so severely as to possibly tempt the Soviet Union into military moves, especially in the oil-vital Middle East.

As to how the immediate crisis will end, no one is sure. Informed sources quoted the West German finance minister as telling a group of German bankers in Bonn that he was confident of a speedy solution. In talks with the U.S. and Bonn's European partners, a tentative scheme for bargaining positions has taken shape, it was reported.

All efforts would be aimed primarily at bringing about a world-wide settlement including the United States and Japan. In this case, West Germany would upvalue the mark in concert with other changes.

Should this effort fail, then a "smaller" European solution would have to be worked out, perhaps by committing all European central banks to stop purchasing dollars in defense of the Smithsonian Agreement. This would be tantamount to a floating en bloc of the Common Market currencies in terms of the dollar and imply a virtual upvaluation of the mark and devaluation of the dollar.

But these sources say West German officials are vehemently opposed to going it alone. They are said to strictly oppose a unilateral upvaluation or float of the mark. (The mark, however, wouldn't be alone if set afloat. The Canadian dollar, the British pound and the Swiss franc are all floating now.)

And, of course, German officials don't have to change the mark if they don't want to. It is considerably more difficult for international money flows to force the upvaluation of a currency than to knock down a weak currency, as happened most recently with the British pound. A central bank defending against upward pressures on its currency can simply issue "printing-press" money to buy dollars. Its potential is unlimited, though inflationary. On the other hand, a central bank defending against weakness has to buy its own currency, using its reserves of foreign exchange and gold. It's bound to run out eventually.

—Charles N. Stabler
—Ray Vicker
—Richard F. Janssen

February 1973

Assessing the Crisis

THE dramatics in the world's money markets go beyond a reshuffling of currency values. It appears that a plan for long-term revision of the monetary system—untested, unaccepted and mostly unrecognized—made its debut during the February 1973 crisis.

And, *mirabile dictu,* it functioned.

Naturally enough, most attention has focused on the sweeping realignment of currency-exchange rates —the turmoil in foreign-exchange markets, the 10% devaluation of the dollar and the unanchoring of the Japanese yen. The concentration has been on numbers: A dollar now buys only 2.9 German marks instead of 3.2, or 6.2 Norwegian krone instead of 6.6, or 60 Spanish pesetas instead of 67.

While most nations, including the U.S., have indicated reasonable satisfaction with the new pattern of rates, uncertainties in the market seem far from ended. For example, the free-market price of gold, a thermometer of apprehension, remains high. Many important currencies are still floating in response to market forces instead of being pegged at agreed values. Most unsettling of all, there has been little outward appearance of progress toward international agreement on a system for making these recurrent monetary upheavals less disruptive.

But some analysts are taking a second, deeper look

at the monetary fireworks, and behind the smoke they discern a surprisingly functional framework. "What we are seeing," says Rimmer de Vries, a vice president and economist at Morgan Guaranty Bank, "is the Volcker plan in action."

And this means the future may be more stable, the analysts say. At a minimum, the U.S. position in negotiations on rebuilding the monetary system will be strengthened.

The so-called Volcker plan, named after Paul Volcker, the jet-set Treasury Under Secretary for Monetary Affairs, is the American proposal for fundamental revision of the world's monetary system. It was first put forth by Treasury Secretary George Shultz at the annual meeting September 1972 of the International Monetary Fund, which runs such things. In November, details were listed in a memorandum to the Committee of 20, the international body saddled with restructuring the way the world manages its monetary affairs. This memorandum was published in the President's annual economic report.

The plan, of course, remains formally nothing more than an American proposal. There is much disagreement about it among other nations, and a good deal of negotiation lies ahead on this and other plans. Most immediately, the financial ministers of the Committee of 20 will meet in Washington, taking up only the initial stages of monetary reform.

But, controversial as the plan is, some of its key elements were put into play in calming the recent crisis. And, without giving all credit to the plan, analysts note that this crisis subsided with vastly less international acrimony, strain and delay than the crisis that ended 14 months earlier with the Smithsonian agreement in realigning exchange rates. "One of the most interesting aspects of the (current) realignment of currency values was the case of implementation relative to the original realignment in December 1971," Alan Greenspan, of the economic consulting firm of Townsend-Greenspan & Co., says.

American officials have made no secret of their effort to use the current crisis to bring about lasting revision. Discussing the realignment at a press conference, Mr. Volcker described it as "helping to reinforce the thrust of a constructive reform of the international monetary system." He added: "We have urged one particular approach toward monetary reform that implies some symmetry, even-handedness of treatment of different countries, different responsibilities for action in different circumstances. In the broadest terms, the kind of action we took and the kind of action the Japanese are taking seems to me consistent with the general thrust of what we've been saying for the longer term."

So what is this "one particular approach"?

First and foremost, the plan is market-oriented. It seeks equilibrium through price adjustments reflecting supply and demand for currencies, rather than erecting ever more restrictive barriers to money flows.

As the most recent crisis boiled, Germany, a long-time defender of free markets, was rapidly building barriers against massive inflows of dollars trying to buy marks. The realignment of rates removes at least for the time being the reason for such inflows by raising the price of marks, rather than blocking the flows by fiat. Similarly, the upward float of Japan's strong currency reduces the pressure of dollar inflows.

Second, the recent action was multilateral, involving the cooperation of major nations. The U.S. cannot devalue its dollar unilaterally because all other currency rates are pegged to it. Other nations could readily offset a dollar devaluation simply by repegging their currencies at the new, lower rate.

Similarly, while other nations can unilaterally change the value of their currencies, their leaders often find such moves politically difficult. For example, a unilateral upward revaluation of the mark, without a similar move by Japan, a major competitor in world markets, would have predictably produced an uproar among Volkswagen workers and in other export industries.

Thus, the realignment had to have the cooperation of many nations. This apparently was achieved in Mr. Volcker's whirlwind tour of major capitals leading up to the devaluation.

Third, the realignment involved the implied threat of penalties against nations whose currencies were undervalued in relation to the economic realities, chiefly the yen and the mark. Such penalties, of course, are a key element in the American proposal.

Most economic analysts say a major weakness of the monetary system devised at Bretton Woods in 1944 is the difficulty of forcing a nation to increase the value of its currency. With an undervalued currency, a nation can stimulate its exports and pile up huge reserves of other currencies through surpluses in its balance of payments; it takes in more money than it pays out.

Under the American proposal, such a nation would be obligated to act to reduce these surpluses, possibly through lowering its barriers to imports from other nations, opening its economy to foreign investment or, finally, revaluing its currency upward. If the nation doesn't make such steps, under the American plan, other nations would have the right to protect themselves by setting up selective tariff barriers or other means. The possibility of such tariff barriers was strongly suggested by U.S. officials in the turbulent days leading up to revaluation of the mark and the float of the yen.

For example, Herbert Stein, chairman of the Council of Economic Advisers, warned preceding the dollar devaluation, "We will have to take our own action if cooperation is not forthcoming." Specifically, he said, an import surcharge was one possibility.

Finally, the U.S. proposes using changes in a nation's monetary reserves as a barometer to indicate when corrective action is needed, before the situation becomes too critical. Increases in reserves of foreign currencies, chiefly the dollar, beyond specified warning points would trigger action to reduce balance of payments surpluses.

A variety of actions are proposed at the discretion of the nation involved. But one key move, a move now being followed by Japan, would be a "transitional float," allowing a currency to rise to a more realistic level and then repegging it.

—CHARLES N. STABLER

February 1973

Monetary Malaise

A MERICAN and European monetary officials are meeting in Paris, with each side apparently hoping the other will spring a secret plan for restoring peace to the world's currency markets.

"If anybody suggests anything, we'll be happy to cooperate," says one U.S. source. But Arthur F. Burns, chairman of the Federal Reserve Board, told Congress that the U.S. doesn't have any firm plan to advance. Rather, Mr. Burns said, he and his colleagues would take to Paris a set of "contingency" reactions to whatever the Europeans propose.

Similarly passive comments come from officials of the Common Market. "Everything depends on what the Americans will do," one European says. He concedes he doesn't have any idea what the Americans will propose. And lack of information on the American position, he suggests, was one reason that finance ministers of the nine Common Market nations couldn't agree on a European approach.

Hope for a breakthrough remains, however. "Richard Nixon likes to govern by surprising the world," one diplomat says.

Ironically, the hurried conferences and consultations of governmental finance officials, the foreign-exchange markets themselves are still functioning with reasonable efficiency. These markets remain closed, but this action just means that central banks won't buy or sell currencies to maintain the alignment of rates agreed to after devaluation of the dollar Feb. 12.

Transactions among commercial banks for themselves and their customers are continuing, both in the spot market and in the market for future sales and purchases. This suggests, one New York banker says, that the best thing the central banks could do for a week or so would be nothing.

"For the time being," he says, "the central banks would be a source of instability." He contends that if central banks begin defending currency values at some artificial alignment, speculators and international companies will open new attacks on whatever currency seems most out of line, generating a new round of instabilities.

The Paris talks bring together authorities from 15 nations. These are the U.S., Japan, Canada, Sweden and Switzerland, plus all nine Common Market countries: West Germany, France, the United Kingdom, Ireland, Italy, Belgium, the Netherlands, Luxembourg and Denmark. The 15th nation is Indonesia, whose foreign minister is chairman of a larger group studying long-range monetary reforms.

The Common Market's preparatory session in Brussels gave the deliberations an inauspicious start, with aides filling in for such finance ministers as Valery Giscard d'Estaing of France, who stuck to his political campaigning in France for coming elections, and for Helmut Schmidt of Germany, who is still nursing his throat after surgery.

Amid the disarray, there appears to be agreement on one point: The present pattern of central, or parity, rates following the 10% devaluation of the dollar Feb. 12 is approximately correct.

What is still unresolved is how to defend these rates

against speculators. The U.S., backing up President Nixon's assertion that the dollar is a "good bet," has indicated it would be willing to intervene in currency markets to support the dollar's worth; indeed, it has made limited support transactions in the past. The major difference between the European and the apparent U.S. position is the degree of American intervention. The Europeans envision a U.S. commitment to more massive intervention than the Nixon administration is willing to give.

Obviously, the administration "wouldn't directly get into any panic" if the U.S. trade position was favored by a slight further rise in European currency rates, one source says.

The basic position of the U.S. emissaries, however, will be that the currency turmoil is a mutual problem. They won't contend, as some Europeans have feared, that it is just a European concern because the main currency speculation is occurring in European markets.

"Clearly both the Europeans and the Americans" are going into the talks "with very serious intentions and a very serious desire to deal with the situation," said Marina Whitman, a member of President Nixon's Council of Economic Advisers, who was in Brussels for a separate meeting with Common Market officials.

But while Europeans agree that the problem requires mutual action, there is little agreement even among themselves about what the action should be.

The West Germans, who have borne the brunt of the speculative assault, want the nine Common Market nations to link their currencies in a united float against the dollar. But France abhors a float, favoring instead technical controls over monetary movements.

Britain, for its part, has said it would be willing to repeg its pound, which has been floating since June 1972. But it has laid down such stringent conditions that few of its Common Market partners are likely to go along. One condition is that if the pound should sink below such a pegged rate, other banks of Common Market nations would give it unlimited support through purchases of that currency. Furthermore, London has sought permission to alter the pound's value should the rate prove out of line. Britain also has asked for assurances that domestic food prices wouldn't be hurt by any monetary moves.

Italy, which has been floating its lira, is believed to want similar assurances. But it has advanced a flexible plan that would allow the currencies to float separately for a while and then to link up ultimately in a common position against the dollar. The virtue of that plan, as the Italians see it, would be its utter confusion; speculators wouldn't know which way to act so they might start betting against one another rather than against governments.

About all the Common Market delegates could agree on in Brussels was a long "shopping list" of suggestions that they could put to the U.S. in Paris. But the "very concrete and positive" suggestions will enable the Common Market countries "to speak with one voice," Belgium's finance minister, Willy de Clercq, said.

The Europeans, it is understood, will question the U.S. about the possibility of Washington's adopting a tighter credit policy and higher interest rates. But such a proposal is likely to get a cool reception from the U.S. delegation, consisting of George P. Shultz, the Treasury Secretary; Paul A. Volcker, the Treasury Under Secretary for Monetary Affairs; and Mr. Burns of the Federal Reserve Board. They will probably contend that an interest-rate rise of one percentage point or two might be big enough to cause major domestic political or economic damage but wouldn't be large enough to entice any dollars home.

A chilly American reaction is also expected to a European request that Washington consider greatly tightening direct controls on the movement of capital out of the U.S. Only weeks ago Mr. Nixon announced his decision to phase out existing restrictions on dollar outflows, and analysts say his aides will be reluctant to add new hurdles to American investing abroad.

Strategists also expect problems concerning U.S. intervention in foreign currency markets. Analysts say limited American intervention had a considerable calming effect in the summer of 1972. But in light of the current, more pessimistic mood, these analysts contend, even massive U.S. market intervention mightn't prove sufficient now.

The Europeans, mindful that the U.S. is relatively poor in gold and almost poverty-stricken in hard foreign currencies, also may sound out U.S. interest in long-term borrowing and perhaps a further increase in the official price of gold. On Feb. 12, 1973, the U.S. proclaimed a new price of $42.22 an ounce, subject to congressional approval.

Once they hear the American answers in Paris, the Common Market members will return to Brussels to deliberate their own course.

If the U.S. makes a large enough "contribution" to a solution, the French presumably could drop their objections to a joint float, especially with their national parliamentary elections behind them. But the Common Market would then still have to contend with the demands of Britain and Italy. If full agreement couldn't be reached with them, the Common Market might then have to fall back on uncoordinated "dirty floats" so called because the member governments would probably intervene to hold currencies within some range acceptable to national goals.

The long-range problem with that, according to one analysis, would be a damaging divisiveness on the international monetary scene. The world could split into three monetary blocs: one tied to the dollar, one linked largely to European currencies and one tied to the Japanese yen.

As viewed by First National City Bank of New York, "this new source of disorder and conflict in international relations casts a long shadow of doubt over the future of world trade and investment—and of the relations between the U.S. and its major allies."

Ideally, the conferees could agree on some plan that could convince speculators that the U.S. and other governments had both the will—and the economic muscle—to defend the pattern of relatively fixed rates set last month. But just as likely, the monetary aides could resign themselves to the need for more meetings and the need to keep official exchange markets closed still longer.

In the limited dealings since most foreign currency exchanges were closed, the dollar has generally drifted lower. And after a spurt of earlier profit taking, bullion prices also advanced against the dollar, rising $1.25 an ounce in London yesterday, to $83.75.

—RICHARD F. JANSSEN

March 1973

Joint Float Emerges

SIX Common Market countries, including France and West Germany, may jointly float their currencies against the U.S. dollar when international monetary markets reopen. But others, notably Britain, may continue to float their own way.

This was the likely result emerging from an emergency meeting March 11, 1973, in Brussels of finance ministers of the nine-nation European Communities.

The Brussels meeting capped a frenetic weekend of activity on the international monetary front. Earlier, representatives of the Free World's major industrial powers met in Paris to search for some way out of the current monetary muddle, which has forced the closing of major foreign-currency exchanges since March 2.

About the only thing the Paris conferees could agree on was to keep markets closed for the time being.

The Common Market representatives, meanwhile, trooped back to the Market's headquarters in Brussels to map their moves. According to sources at the Brussels talks, the ministers were leaning toward a "partial joint float." As conceived, the currencies of France, West Germany, Belgium, the Netherlands, Denmark and Luxembourg would be pegged closely against each other but would be allowed to float as a bloc against the dollar. Britain, which has been floating by itself since last June, would probably continue to float independently, against both the dollar and against the six in the joint float.

Ireland, which has pretty much linked its currency to the floating pound, would probably continue that relationship, thereby also floating separately or with the six.

Italy, whose lira has also been floating, still hadn't decided what it would do. Its officials debated whether to float separately or with the six.

To help keep the six jointly floating currencies in line, sources said, the participating member countries were contemplating a pool of currencies and gold equivalent to $10 billion. This fund would be tapped to grant one-year credits at low-interest rates to help prop participating currencies that threatened to sink too low in relation to other currencies in the bloc.

Under previous Common Market policy, the member countries had agreed to hold their currencies within 2% of each other, half the band allowed under the general rule of the International Monetary Fund.

Monetary experts at the Brussels meeting said that other European nations might also join in the joint float. These outsiders might include Switzerland, Sweden, Norway, Finland and Austria.

The Gaullists' success in the run-off French election is believed to have made possible French support for the joint float. The arrangement would be broadly welcomed by the Nixon administration, but isn't without a major peril. If the six float up too much against the dollar, France would push for a special tax on imports from outsiders.

With this "trade war" threat as leverage, the Europeans hope the U.S. will yet agree to some form of help to keep the dollar from going down too much relative to their floating bloc. U.S. sources also worry that the European bloc could be used in a "dirty float" downward and rob the U.S. of the trade advantage sought from two dollar devaluations.

The decision to keep exchanges closed has actually more technical than practical significance. With the closing, the world's major powers simply stated that they wouldn't intervene on their local markets to support the value of their currencies against the dollar.

Banks still generally trade currencies with other banks and offer to buy and sell foreign money to meet customer demands. Volume has slowed because speculators and businessmen are reluctant to venture out with major commitments that can be postponed. Some monetary costs also have climbed for importers and exporters.

By and large, however, the multibillion-dollar international trade still goes on. And tourists can still swap dollars for marks or francs, though they may run into some merchants looking for quick profit on an innocent abroad.

The Paris meeting brought together an expanded version of the Group of 10, a long-dormant unit of major powers within the 125-nation International Monetary Fund.

The group includes the U.S., Canada, Japan and Sweden, plus six members of the Common Market: Britain, France, West Germany, Italy, the Netherlands and Belgium. These were augmented by the three other Common Market countries, Denmark, Ireland and Luxembourg, plus Switzerland and officials of the IMF, Common Market, Organization for Economic Cooperation and Development and Bank for International Settlements. Indonesia, too, sat in as chairman of another group mapping monetary reform.

The wider Paris session followed the script suggested by the more pessimistic experts: The Europeans said they couldn't decide anything until they knew what the U.S. would do to help. And U.S. Treasury Secretary George P. Shultz said that first the U.S. would have to know exactly what the Europeans could agree on among themselves. The result: "They agreed to disagree," said one U.S. aide.

Mr. Shultz put it more politely, telling a 10 p.m. news conference at the U.S. Embassy in Paris that there were "procedural conclusions" but "no substantive conclusions."

The procedure agreed upon was that the finance ministers would have their deputies make "a technical study" of measures that the ministers could decide upon when they meet again in Paris. The goal is "to make it possible" for European countries to officially reopen their exchange markets next Monday, the communique said.

The reopening will have to come without the U.S. having accepted any of the major suggestions advanced by the Europeans, Mr. Shultz made clear. The 20 questions put to the U.S. by the Common Market amounted to three main points, all of which Mr. Shultz politely but clearly rejected.

On whether the U.S. will engineer higher interest rates to lure back dollars from abroad, Mr. Shultz told reporters that America's interest-rate policy will be made "in the context of our domestic economic development."

The European question on whether the U.S. will impose tight legal controls on capital outflows reflects "misunderstanding," he said. It remains our intention "to phase out existing controls by the end of 1974," he reaffirmed, and he argued that contrary to the general impression, the flow of long-term private capital "in the last four or five years" has been from Europe to the U.S.

As to the U.S. agreeing to "intervene" by purchasing excess dollars to stabilize currency prices, Mr. Shultz declared: "We have undertaken no commitment to intervene." That isn't the same as saying, he added, that "we wouldn't intervene under any circumstances."

The U.S. did do some experimental purchasing of dollars for foreign currencies last summer and again early this year. But aides say the U.S. couldn't afford to make massive enough dealings to offset the immense amounts of speculation lately. Moreover, they argue, an agreement to intervene would amount to restoring "convertibility" of the dollar into other reserve assets, a plum they want to withhold until the Europeans agree to long-range trade and monetary rule changes.

All did agree the "crisis was due to speculative movement of funds which has occurred even though agreed central rates correspond" with "the economic requirements," the communique said. The nations involved "unanimously expressed their determination to ensure jointly an orderly exchange rate system," it went on. "But don't confuse 'orderly' with fixed rates," one insider cautioned, explaining that some governments deem floating rates more orderly than fixed ones, and that a polyglot combination of currency practices may be the only possible near-term course.

The meeting at the Paris office of the Washington-based IMF took place with a maximum of ministerial showmanship that added to the crisis atmosphere.

Although they were all going to the same place for lunch, the ministers traveled in individual limousines with national flags flying, escorted by klaxon-sounding squads of motorcycle police. Dozens of white-helmeted, red-braided gendarmes brusquely shoved around lesser aides and reporters, who had to wait in the chilly street outside most of the day. But for about six hours prior to the French Finance Minister Valery Giscard d'Estaing's press conference that night, newsmen were gathered into a palatial French government building and treated to cocktails and canapes by tailcoated waiters.

Despite the image of urgency, if not chaos, however, Mr. Shultz said there isn't any reason "to get yourself into a state of alarm." Despite the "fair amount of turmoil" in the past two years, "world trade has continued to expand," national economies are "generally strong," and a spirit of "goodwill" exists, he said.

March 1973

Monetary System Fades

WITH key world currencies afloat against the U.S. dollar, and likely to continue floating for some time, the international monetary system has dissolved into a formless suspension of regional blocs and isolated outsiders.

But monetary specialists, while generally agreeing with this assessment, differ sharply on the consequences for world trade.

C. A. Costanzo, executive vice president of First National City Bank in New York, says he, for one, has "never been frightened by floating rates." In his view, "people have more confidence in market rates than fixed rates."

But A. Robert Abbood, executive vice president of First National Bank of Chicago, cautions a float is inherently perilous. "What worries me is what might happen if there is some major event, in Britain or the Middle East, that could encourage speculations."

With such a danger, banks will be cautious about participating in transactions calling for the delivery of currencies at some future date. "The cost of forward cover is already substantial and it may prove prohibitive," he asserts, and this could prove burdensome for companies in international trade that want to protect themselves against currency fluctuations.

"The end of Bretton Woods," as West German Fi-

nance Minister Helmut Schmidt described it, came
early March 11, 1973, at a meeting in Brussels of the
nine-nation Common Market. Under the Bretton Woods
accord, negotiated in New Hampshire in 1944, all foreign currencies were pegged in terms of the dollar, and
the dollar was pegged against gold and convertible into
bullion.

The Bretton Woods system actually started wither-
ing in August 1971, when President Nixon halted all
further gold sales from the U.S. Treasury. It atrophied a
bit more in subsequent months as the currencies of
Britain, Canada, Japan, Ireland and Italy were un-
leashed to float their own separate ways.

But the coffin was sealed and buried early yester-
day morning. Under the Common Market pact, West
Germany, France, Belgium, Luxembourg, the Netherlands and Denmark pledged to link their currencies
within 2¼% of each other and let them float as a bloc
against the dollar.

To prevent the West German mark from pulling its
floating partners up too sharply, the Bonn government
lifted the value of its currency by 3%. The Netherlands
and Belgium, with close ties to the German economy,
said they were considering similar moves.

Of the other Common Market nations, Britain and
Ireland indicated they would continue floating in tan-
dem against both their six Common Market allies and
the dollar. Italy, too, decided to go its own way.

Some other nations may join with the Common
Market six in the float, most notably Sweden, Norway,
Switzerland and Austria, but Austria, for one, was holding off any action until major international currency
exchanges reopen their doors next Monday, for the first
time in over two weeks.

What position the U.S. now will take in the ex-
tended monetary muddle remains unclear. "One ingre-

dient has been put into place," said Paul A. Volcker, U.S. Treasury Under Secretary for Monetary Affairs, of the Common Market's joint float. But when asked in Brussels to explain the other necessary ingredients, he responded, "That's what we are talking about here."

U.S. banking sources say they expect the Nixon administration to agree tacitly to support the dollar's value through more extensive intervention on foreign exchange markets. As one banking source enunciates the expected U.S. stance: "Officially, we say we believe the dollar is stable but we don't rule out intervention from time to time. Then we'll go ahead and do it. In other words, we're saying we're willing to live together with Europe but not get married."

Officials on both sides of the Atlantic expect the float to be "dirty": that is, they expect governments to intervene on currency markets to keep the floating currencies within desired bounds.

Common Market officials indicated, however, they hadn't decided on the mechanics of their float and the intervention that would be used to keep the six floaters within 2¼% of each other. French authorities indicated they were considering measures to strengthen already stiff currency controls.

Japan, which has been floating its yen independently since the U.S. devalued the dollar 10% on Feb. 12, 1973, was expected to continue to closely regulate the yen's fluctuations when markets reopen. But the Japanese currency may well be allowed to float higher than the West German mark against the dollar.

March 1973

Cooling Off the Money Crisis

PARADOXICAL though it may seem, the adoption of floating rates by all the major trading countries is likely to bring a greater degree of tranquility to the international monetary system than it has seen for several years. The long series of monetary upheavals that started with the devaluation of the pound in 1967 may at last be coming to an end.

This optimistic prognosis is not based merely on the fact that, with floating rates nearly universal, any further change will have to be in the direction of less flexibility of exchange rates. In fact, it is by no means obvious that the floating exchange rates will be subject to much fluctuation; the U.S.-Canadian dollar exchange has hardly moved at all since the Canadian dollar was floated nearly three years ago. Other floating currencies, especially the pound, have shown somewhat more volatility, but the exchange rate between the U.S. dollar and the six continental currencies is more likely to follow the U.S.-Canadian pattern.

There are three main reasons for expecting that international monetary affairs will gradually move from the front page to the financial page of our daily newspapers. The first reason is that the defenders of fixed exchange rates should by now have realized the futility of their last-ditch fight and may find some merit in floating after all. Except for Canada, which has a long

history of floating, four other countries that adopted
floating rates during the last few months (Britain,
Switzerland, Italy and Japan) did so reluctantly, but
having tried it, they liked it. Britain's only regret appears to be that it did not adopt floating 15 years ago, in
which case its recent history might well have been less
depressing. The other three, for reasons of their own,
will probably find it difficult to go back to a fixed rate,
although in the case of Japan the float is so "dirty" that
it probably would not make much difference if it did.
Among the six most recent converts, Germany and Holland already had some previous experience with floating rates, while Belgium had been running a dual rate
system. It is mainly M. Giscard d'Estaing who now has
to eat his golden words.

The second reason for expecting greater tranquility
is the greatly improved competitive position of the
United States. For a while it looked as if we had not
gained any trade benefits from the devaluation of 1971.
Now that the December, 1972, trade figures have been
revised and the January trade figures have shown further improvement, there are indications that we may
have turned the corner. The large trade deficit of 1972
resulted from a sharp increase in imports combined
with initial sluggishness in our exports. From the middle of 1972, however, our exports have shown new vigor,
and in January, 1973, they were running at an unprecedented annual rate of nearly $60 billion. One should not
give too much weight to one month's figures, but the
upward trend is unmistakable.

It is too early to say how much of the gain in exports is due to our devaluation and superior domestic
price performance, how much to improved economic
conditions abroad, and how much to special circumstances such as the worldwide grain shortage. All of
these factors have probably played a part, but since

they may be with us for some time, the outlook for our exports is favorable. The rise in the value of our imports reflects partly the strong recovery in our economy, partly the higher cost of imports due to devaluation. Our growth rate will probably taper off somewhat and the devaluation effect is of a once-and-for-all nature, though of course repeated this year. On balance we are likely to see a significantly smaller trade deficit in 1973, accompanied by some improvements in other items of the balance of payments.

The third reason is that the dollar has come through all these crises stronger than ever. Its exchange value in terms of other currencies has been reduced, but no substitute for its predominant role in world finance has so far appeared, and none is on the horizon as long as members of the European Economic Community cannot agree among themselves. All the brave talk about dethroning the dollar, for instance, by going back to gold, has come to nothing.

If the expectation of an improved U.S. balance of payments is realized it also means that we can now begin to de-emphasize the policy of "benign neglect" which we have been pursuing for the last four years, and which has been crowned with considerable success. This policy, first formulated by a Republican pre-election task force in 1968 under the chairmanship of Professor Gottfried Haberler of Harvard, was aimed at forcing a depreciation of our overvalued dollar. At that time there was no possibility of devaluing the dollar unilaterally, since several other countries had made it clear they would devalue by an equal amount, thus nullifying our move. These countries therefore had to be persuaded by a continuing accumulation of inconvertible dollar balances.

It was not an easy policy to carry through; for one thing, it could not be publicly explained and therefore was widely misunderstood not only abroad but also by several influential newspapers in the U.S. It put a considerable strain on the international monetary system, and even so results were slow in coming.

The drastic actions taken by John Connally while he was Secretary of the Treasury were a departure from the tactics, though not the strategy, of benign neglect. His successor, George Shultz, wisely returned to the previous approach; thus reports of the recent meeting in Paris quoted him as responding to European pressures for higher U.S. interest rates by saying that our interest rates are determined by domestic considerations. Such statements are the essence of benign neglect, and so was the announcement that we will phase out our capital control programs by the end of 1974. At the same time it appears that by avoiding his predecessor's strong-arm methods, Secretary Shultz has preserved international harmony.

From this rather sanguine interpretation of recent events it should not be inferred, however, that the millennium is now at hand. Although recent experience with floating rates has been favorable, they may raise more serious problems in the longer run. Importers, exporters and bankers can probably live with them, since they can generally hedge their exchange risks, but the effect on direct investment may not be so innocuous. There is at present also a huge volume of "hot money" whose movement may at times be destabilizing. Consequently the search for a more stable international monetary system should not be abandoned; to arrive at such a system was indeed a second purpose of the strategy of benign neglect. Secretary Shultz made a fair and comprehensive proposal to this effect at the IMF meeting last September, but until last week it apparently created little enthusiasm among other countries. This proposal was intended to preserve the good features of the

Bretton Woods system while making it more responsive
to changing economic conditions. Now that the fixed-
rate die-hards have at last had to admit defeat, the
prospects for durable reform may have suddenly improved, and the pressure for reform will become over-
whelming if universal floating rates turn out to be un-
manageable. But whether or not floating rates will last,
we are now much closer to international economic equilibrium than we have been for a long time. Provided we
continue to pursue a responsible fiscal policy and keep
our monetary policy on a more even keel, we may have
confidence in the maintenance of an open world economy.

—HENDRIK S. HOUTHAKKER
Harvard University

March 1973

The Enduring Lure of Gold

"AMERICA'S position concerning gold is being proved absolutely wrong by events," says an official of one of Switzerland's Big Three banks. He shakes his head as he adds: "If the American government had doubled the price of gold in 1968 instead of establishing a two-tier market, you now would have a strong dollar and the world would be better off."

There is a self-assured sound in his voice as he speaks with I-told-you-so eloquence. Being proved right seems of more concern than the substantial amounts which the portfolio department of this bank has invested in the declining American stock market.

Only time will tell whether the world's gold bugs or its equally dogmatic anti-gold nuts will be proved right on monetary matters. But, judging by the way the free gold price has climbed above $100 an ounce, the gold bugs have more grounds for chortling than do advocates of managed cellulose pulp currencies. Today, gold is anything but dead as a store of wealth. This is one of the roles for which money has been created, of course, a role which the United States dollar finds harder and harder to fill.

The free market price of gold started 1973 at $64.90 an ounce on the London Gold Market. Since then it has soared far above the level that even the most vociferous

.gloom and doom gold bugs had been predicting when viewing the world through their black glasses at the year's start.

Gold's resilience provides warning lights to the difficulties facing any easy revamping of the world's monetary system along lines advocated by present occupants of the U.S. Treasury and the White House. This may portend all kinds of troubles ahead, too. Confidence in the U.S. dollar has not been restored, and events in Washington raise doubts about America's ability to restore it. The nearly $100 billion overhang of U.S. dollars in overseas hands becomes an ever heavier leaden weight upon what is left of the world monetary system.

When this is coupled with a growing feeling of economic and political mismanagement in Washington, reasons for the present gold rush start coming into focus. To foreigners, Watergate, wild inflation, the dollar overhang, a protectionist Congress and the energy gap merge into a picture of an America which doesn't know where it is going. And many people in Washington seem less concerned about that than they are about bringing down the captain on the U.S. bridge, even though the ship is taking on water dangerously all the while.

In simple economic terms, gold's price is soaring because a lot of people abroad think that if the American ship is foundering, then an ounce of gold at more than $100 is worth more than a hundred of those green pieces of paper with George Washington's picture on its face.

Devaluation of the dollar in terms of gold might be a good thing in the long term. The trouble is this devaluation is uncontrolled, not an action taken by the U.S. government or by governments in concert. It is occurring as a conspicuous show of lack of confidence in the dollar and in the people who have been managing it in Washington.

Ironically, the U.S. missed an opportunity in March 1968 to maintain control of gold. At that time a rush of speculators and gold hoarders poured $3 billion into gold, upsetting the carefully managed pool which had been maintained by world central bankers to keep gold's price at $35 an ounce. Markets were shut down. World central bankers gathered in Washington to analyze the situation.

Britain's Lord O'Brien, governor of the Bank of England, suggested that America double the monetary price of gold. This would have permitted the gold-dollar monetary system to resume control of gold at the new price. The dollar would have been the world's kingpin currency for a while longer. From hindsight one could conclude that this might have prevented many of the monetary ills which subsequently developed in the system.

Any gold price increase in 1968 might have led to another and another, with no real benefits of enduring stability. However, a doubling of the gold price would have increased the world total of international reserves to a level of about $115 billion. And gold would have composed two-thirds of those reserves, a figure that would have been more than enough to correct the weaknesses of the dollar which then were apparent. By failing to act when the opportunity was presented, doubts about the dollar were allowed to grow and then to mushroom.

Some support for the British proposal came from other Europeans at the meeting. But America's representatives were adamant. Gold was to be phased out from the monetary system over a period of time. The Special Drawing Right or paper gold would become the new unit to provide a base for the monetary system.

Raise the monetary price of gold? No sir. That would benefit those wicked South Africans and the Communists in the Soviet Union, since South Africa and the USSR are the largest producers of gold. It was popular then for America to take moralistic positions on economic and political matters even at a cost to the U.S. This, of course, was the same attitude that helped get the U.S. into Vietnam.

Moreover, any monetary gold price hike would be inflationary, U.S. officials warned. So that was out.

The monetary price was to be held at $35 an ounce while the free price would be allowed to find its own level. This it most certainly did.

Since that time the U.S. has twice raised the hypothetical monetary price of gold to the present $42.22 an ounce. But the price on the free market is more than two and a half times that level. And that price still is rising.

As for those wicked South Africans and those Red Russians? All of the gold they don't keep in reserves is being sold on the free market, at hefty prices far above that $70 an ounce monetary price which Lord O'Brien had advocated in 1968.

As for inflation? The damage had already been done through pumping billions of dollars worth of superfluous dollars into the world's economic bloodstream. As if this wasn't enough, world monetary managers created the equivalent of over $9 billion in SDRs and expanded International Monetary Fund drawing rights to compound the monetary-inspired inflation. Since that 1968 conference which established the two-tier gold market, the total liquidity of IMF countries doubled, and the world has been on a wild inflationary binge.

Is the world any closer to an SDR-based monetary system? Hardly. Those $9 billion in SDRs in use today are only a drop in the bucket beside the nearly $100 billion in overseas hands which seem less and less attractive to holders.

Moreover, now noises are coming from the Middle East concerning the possible creation of a gold-backed dinar by oil-rich Arab nations. It would be a complex task to create such a currency. Complexities may not be any greater than that for creating a very substantial total of SDRs or something similar. The way Arab nations are piling up oil money, their gold-backed dinar may prove ever more appealing in the period ahead. And may make the SDR less appealing in many parts of the world.

Which would you choose if you had the choice? A gold-backed dinar, or an SDR? When this question is asked, it becomes apparent that a gold-backed dinar would create a new element in the monetary arena, one which would probably raise all kinds of problems for the SDR. Arabs by nature trust gold more than they trust paper currencies or substitutes, (and who can blame them?) so they may not be in any hurry to put their trust in such devices. Switzerland certainly isn't. This little country with its sound currency has elected to scorn the SDR in its monetary dealings.

The energy situation intrudes into the picture, too. Western Europe has even more cause for concern than has America in this respect since it imports a greater percentage of its energy needs. Europe's energy needs plus its respect for gold provides two reasons why it might be easy for Europe and the Arab world to reach a rapport in the present troubled state of affairs.

Only a year ago the prestigious Bank for International Settlements in Basel was warning that the world would split into money blocs if something wasn't done to resolve problems of the inconvertible dollar. Those blocs could be America on the one hand and Europe with Arab lands on the other if America's political and economic cards are handled as crudely as were its ploys during its period of benign neglect of the world's monetary system. Japan might form a third bloc in its part of the world.

Meanwhile, the Nixon administration and Congress proceed blithely toward a new tax bill without any regard to how actions are being interpreted abroad. Proposals would revamp taxes paid by U.S. corporations and citizens abroad. In a reasoned analysis, a tax expert of the influential London Financial Times scored the U.S. tax proposals.

Said he: "They are a deliberate attempt by the Americans to skim off more than their share of the total tax revenue to be derived from international business activities, and are therefore bound to provoke retaliation by other countries."

In other areas such as trade, Europeans become more and more concerned about the protectionist attitude being displayed by sources in Washington. As fears of possible trade wars develop, the desire to hold gold instead of dollars increases. Any trade war is more likely to lead to a recession than to general prosperity, thus increasing gold's allure.

That, of course, also decreases the attractiveness of the SDR. And if the SDR is going to have trouble replacing the dollar in international dealings, what would take its place? It is obvious that a lot of people are betting that gold will play this role.

A strong theoretical position can be made against gold, drawing upon the bitter experiences the world has had with the gold standard in the past. In the final analysis, gold is nothing but a yellow metal to which men have accorded a value. If it seems silly to deify gold, you may term the gold lover a "gold bug" or a "nut" or anything else. It doesn't disturb the economic factors one iota, though it may increase your sense of superiority vis-a-vis the gold bug.

Instead of fighting gold as an evil metal to cut from the monetary system at all costs, America should be examining how to use gold to further its own interests. We do have around 275 million ounces of gold at Fort Knox and in the Federal Reserve Bank of New York vaults. If Arabs think so much of gold, and we need oil so badly, maybe the thing to do is to place a $200 an ounce value on our gold.

That would automatically provide us with $55 billion worth to sell to interested parties, rather than the $11.6 billion on hand at $42.22 per ounce. America's balance of payments situation as it dickers for foreign oil would be vastly improved.

Any such thought may be only a hypothetical exercise to suggest possibilities. It does seem, however, that American policy makers should be paying more attention to how gold could be utilized as an ally of American policy rather than to waste any more time fighting it as if it were a monetary cancer to remove.

Before long, however, Arabs are likely to establish oil prices to a gold tie which would automatically increase petroleum prices were gold's price raised. This only goes to show that perhaps America may already have lost all control of gold because of its dogmatic opposition to the yellow metal.

This doesn't mean, however, that gold's price is going to stagnate merely because the U.S. wishes that it would. It merely means that monetarily the U.S. may be buffeted by circumstances in the period ahead rather than acting rationally to control its own destiny.

Now with the free gold price over the $100 an ounce barrier, one is reminded of the advice George Bernard Shaw gave in his "An Intelligent Woman's Guide to Socialism."

Said he: "You have to choose between trusting to the natural stability of gold, and the honesty and intelligence of members of the government. And with due respect for these gentlemen, I would advise you, as long as the capitalistic system lasts, to vote for gold."

—RAY VICKER

May 1973

Learning to Float

THE world monetary system is suffering from nervous dollar palpitations, its backbone of fixed exchange rates has been broken and it is wracked by gold fever.

But it's still very much in business.

That's the relieved finding of top bankers and financial officials at the international monetary conference of the American Bankers Association in Paris this June 1973. Looking beyond the day-to-day turmoil of international exchange markets, they see an underlying structure that so far hasn't seriously impaired trade and investment among nations.

"Despite the phantoms and ghosts that were forecast (when the 25-year-old Bretton Woods system of fixed exchange rates collapsed three months ago), the present situation has proved perfectly workable," says G. Morris Dorrance, chairman of Philadelphia National Bank. However, he and other analysts warn that a long period of recuperation lies ahead for the monetary system, a period in which world trade and investment may yet suffer from sudden currency gyrations and stifling protectionist controls.

The present system of exchanging national currencies, which isn't really a "system" at all, developed in disorderly fashion after devaluation of the dollar Feb.

12, 1973, the second reduction in the dollar's exchange
rate in 14 months. Previously, most national currencies
had been pegged in value in terms of the dollar, and
until suspension of gold convertibility in August 1971,
the dollar had been pegged to gold. Now, in sharp contrast to the old system, the dollar is floating against
other currencies—a situation that generates uncertainty about its future value.

For years central bankers and government officials
have warned that such uncertainties would hamper
world trade and discourage investment, to the detri-
ment of national economies. And despite the surprising
serviceability of the present system, that danger is still
very much a reality, most bankers agree. A more formal
restructuring of the system is still needed, they contend, and moves in this direction are being pushed forward.

But in the meantime, they are learning to cope
with the float.

"People have learned to live with it," says John
Francis Prideaux, chairman of National Westminster
Bank Ltd., one of Britain's biggest banks. Short-term
international transactions haven't suffered, he says.
But he adds: "I don't think it (the float) would be good
as a long-term thing. If you are a manufacturer of
heavy electrical equipment making delivery over, say, a
five- or six-year period, it really is an impediment to
business. You have to hire a foreign-exchange expert
when your business really is making electrical equipment."

That's a typical assessment, according to talks with
bankers in the luxurious meeting rooms and corridors
of Paris's expensive hotels and at multicourse meals in
such settings as the Presidential Palace and a former
prison once occupied by Marie Antoinette. They say the
float has had little impact on short-term transactions.

But the present system has been less benign on longer-term contracts and on investment, especially in light of the controls that many nations have imposed on capital movements across their borders.

"I don't see any slowing of trade" because of uncertainties and controls, says A. W. Clausen, president of Bank of America, "but investment is a horse of another color."

The float apparently is more of a concern for European businessmen than for Americans. It's a rare American banker who reports any slowdown in trade by his customers. But European bankers say their clients are getting edgy.

"Our customers feel very uncomfortable and have felt that way especially during the last few weeks," says Tore Bronwald, chairman of Svenska Handelsbanken, a large Stockholm commercial bank. "The daily helpings of uncertainty and changes are making them doubtful about the float."

In large part, however, these concerns appear to be based not so much on the fact of floating as on the steep decline in the dollar's value in recent weeks. The overall drop in the dollar's value has, of course, made U.S. goods tougher competitors in world markets.

Some analysts say one immediate result of the float, for good or ill, is a third devaluation of the dollar, amounting to 7%. In contrast to previous currency realignments, however, this change in value was managed by supply-and-demand forces in foreign-exchange markets, rather than by hurried conferences in world capitals by finance ministers and central bankers.

And it is being accomplished without the air of crisis and without the heavy capital movements of past currency changes. Because most central banks are refraining from large intervention in the markets, they haven't piled up massive new dollar holdings. In the cri-

sis of the summer of 1972, some $6 billion flowed out of
the U.S. into foreign central banks, and in February
1973 the outflow was $8 billion. In the present turbu-
lence, these outflows are estmiated at less than $1 bil-
lion.

"The floating-rate system worked pretty well in the
face of the uncertainties of recent weeks," U.S. Treasury
Secretary George Shultz told a press conference. "It's a
reasonable system as we try to negotiate broader economic reform."

There is a widespread feeling at the Paris meeting
among private bankers as well as U.S. officials, that the
market may have overdone its reduction in the value of
the dollar. The outlook for the U.S. balance of payments
—the flow of money into and out of the nation—is regarded as generally more favorable this year than in recent years, and this is expected to strengthen the dollar
in months to come.

Significantly, Walter B. Wriston, chairman of First
National City Bank of New York, says he can't find any
takers for a bet he wants to make. The bet: That the
dollar will appreciate in value over the next 24 months
against any currency you want to name.

While the floating-rate system has taken the steam
out of what would have been another dollar crisis under
the old system, some bankers note that this hasn't been
accomplished free. "This seemingly easy way of handling (currency-rate changes) does involve a cost," says
Knut Getz Wold, governor of the central bank of Norway. "This is the difficulty of the present system, but
the hope is that it is a transitional one."

The cost comes about through wider fluctuations
in currency prices than under the previous system and
through increases in the cost of trading in futures markets, where importers and exporters insure themselves
against losses from exchange-rate changes. To protect

themselves against the uncertainties of future values, foreign-exchange traders have widened the spread between the price at which they will sell currencies for future delivery and the price they are willing to pay. This move increases the cost of hedging, which is buying one currency and selling another for future delivery in order to come out even on a trade deal that involves payment for goods in the future.

In some cases, of course, these costs may be translated into higher prices for consumers. "The producers won't take the fluctuations," says Emilio G. Collado, executive vice president of Exxon Corp. International oil companies have agreed to Arab oil nations' demands that they refigure the price of oil every month to reflect possible declines in the purchasing power of the dollar. This costly new pact is "a fruit of devaluation, of changes in the exchange structure," Mr. Collado says.

But not all foreign sellers are in such a strong position to demand protection against constantly changing currency values. "You take a French aircraft company that signed contracts in dollars to deliver planes two or three years ahead," a leading French banker laments. "Competition keeps it from demanding more dollars for the same planes while it takes more dollars to buy the francs needed to meet payrolls here. The ultimate loss grows almost daily as the planes take shape."

Aside from the mixed effects on trade and investment, the float also is having an impact on efforts to achieve a more lasting and formal restructuring of the monetary system. These efforts have been under way for a long time, mainly in the so-called Committee of 20 of the International Monetary Fund, which administers what is left of the system set up at Bretton Woods after World War II. The committee, which represents major nations but also has some representation from less-developed ones, had sought to agree on broad recommendations prior to the next meeting of the IMF in Nairobi in September 1973. Now, that timetable, never very certain, appears even less so.

One reason is the recent spectacular run-up in the price of gold, bankers say. This price rise is partly a result of defensive controls over the movements of currency that many countries have established. These controls make it difficult to switch from weak currencies into strong ones, leaving gold as an attractive alternative. And the increases reflect, as well, many investors' disenchantment with any currency.

The result is to stiffen the resolve of some European officials to resist U.S. efforts to eliminate gold as any part of the future monetary system. In fact, some bankers here say there have been recent secretive soundings among European negotiators about the possibility of sharply raising the official price of gold to $200 an ounce; the present official price is $42.22. That would put the official price well above the present market price.

The float, with its apparent serviceability, also has tended to diminish the role of the IMF as an administrator of the monetary system, some bankers say; the system it was set up to administer no longer exists, they note.

Moreover, the crisis-free operation of the floating monetary system is diminishing the sense of urgency among many bankers and government authorities for a speedy overhaul of the monetary structure. Their comments here indicate a growing "wait-and-see" attitude toward changing the formal rules of the system.

"I think it would be a mistake to rush into any agreement" on restructuring the monetary system, says Roy L. Reierson, senior vice president and economist for Crocker International Bank of New York. "I think the passage of time will provide some important experience in the operation of the system as it is. It will enable us to make a more accurate appraisal of floating currencies. We need to know how effective they are."

Similarly, Otmar Emminger, deputy governor of the German central bank, says the operation of the exchange markets under floating rates and other economic trends may be more important in determining the ultimate shape of a revised monetary system than the technical negotiations under the IMF's sponsorship. Whether the world can ever return to fixed currency rates is less dependent on "rules and regulations" written by negotiators than on a restoration of a strong dollar and more effective anti-inflation efforts by industrialized nations, Mr. Emminger says.

U.S. officials, while still officially expressing hope for some kind of general monetary agreement in time for the IMF's meeting in Kenya's capital, also appear less concerned with speed now that the floating system seems workable. "We certainly don't want to make an agreement just to make an agreement," says Paul A. Volcker, Under Secretary of the Treasury for Monetary Affairs. But "we ought to keep trying for what we can do" by the time of the Nairobi meeting, even though there is little expectation of a detailed agreement that soon, he says.

Some bankers are worried by such relaxed attitudes toward the system through which world trade and investment flow. For example, Leslie C. Peacock, president of San Francisco's Crocker National Bank, thinks these attitudes reflect a false sense of security.

"The world has started on a wrong course, and its evolution, I suspect, will be very adverse," he warns. Because a government won't let free-market forces swing its currency's value far from what is best for its domestic economy, the absence of fixed rates is leading the world into a period of restrictions, he fears. This, he says, could leave the 1960s looking like "the golden era of freedom" in world commerce.

Both these bankers who are worried about the float and those who are more sanguine agree on one forecast: Whatever more formal structure is decided on by negotiators, the float will be a part of any future international monetary system. It will be used they predict, as a transitional measure to allow a currency to find a realistic level in the market before it is formally pegged to some fixed value.

"A temporary float may be a very good instrument" in the future monetary system, says Wolfgang Schmitz, president of the Austrian central bank.

—JAMES P. GANNON
—RICHARD F. JANSSEN
—CHARLES N. STABLER

June 1973

Intervention in the Float

WORLD monetary authorities are having as much trouble agreeing among themselves about what to do right away as they are on deciding about a new monetary system for the future.

A dispute over whether to step immediately into the "floating" currency markets emerged in June 1973, as about 200 top bankers and officials milled around during the American Bankers Association International Monetary Conference and the partly overlapping ministerial meeting of the 24-nation Organization for Economic Cooperation and Development.

A sense that something might be done to stem the decline of the dollar developed when French Finance Minister Valery Giscard d'Estaing called at an OECD session for all countries to support their currency parities "within the next few days."

Setting such a deadline seemed reasonable, observers said, in light of mounting complaints by Continental businessmen that U.S. exports had gained a further 6% or 7% price edge through the dollar's downward float since the 10% formal devaluation in February 1973. Moreover, top U.S. officials were openly agreeing the dollar had gone down too far. Some strategists were arguing the best time to give it a boost back upward is at a time, as occured in mid-June, in which market forces were starting to move that way anyhow.

But, it appeared the French deadline would go unheeded. The major reason, insiders explain, is West Germany is dead set against such intervention for domestic reasons. In heated private exchanges, German officials argued with other European officials that it would worsen West German inflation if German marks were spent, either by Germany or the U.S., to buy excess dollars. Under the "snake" agreement in which eight European currencies are floating jointly against the dollar, a decision to intervene to affect that float has to be unanimous, sources said, so even one holdout could block the French-sought move.

Nor are Nixon administration officials eager to resume intervention, which was the main means of steadying values under the old fixed-rate system. "We haven't taken any obligation to intervene," Paul A. Volcker, Treasury Under Secretary for Monetary Affairs, reiterated to reporters. But such action in the interest of "orderly" markets isn't ruled out.

Mr. Volcker's comments came shortly after Mr. Giscard d'Estaing repeated his call at the closing luncheon of the bankers meeting. In that speech, the French minister seemed to soften his proposal, saying it would "particularly help" if "some initiatives were taken in the next few days, notably on the part of the large nations whose currencies have been recently under attack."

As to longer-run negotiations toward a new monetary system, Mr. Giscard d'Estaing heartened U.S. officials by what appeared to be a conciliatory stand, putting emphasis on the broad points of agreement. These include parities that are stable but more readily adjustable than in the old system, and "convertibility" of excess holdings into some other asset, such as gold or the

Special Drawing Rights created by the 125-country International Monetary Fund. "I liked the tone," Mr. Volcker said.

But in both private and open discussions, U.S. and key European officials agreed enormous differences remain on precise features, further slowing the already-lengthy negotations. For instance, Europeans have all but rejected the idea currency rate changes should be triggered by an "objective indicator" such as the level of a nation's reserves. Nixon aides argue this is vital to assure fair treatment for all countries.

Technical as such issues sound, the financial officials are increasingly noting they involve political fundamentals such as sovereignty. The U.S., for instance, is "skeptical," Mr. Volcker says, of putting "a very high degree of discretionary authority" in the IMF. This stance reflects a spreading concern among negotiators, insiders say, that any system they come up with fast may also break down rapidly because governments will break the new rules.

To achieve only "a semblance of reform" would be "an expedient as nefarious in the long-run as the present situation," Mr. Giscard d'Estaing said, warning "it would spell the certain destruction of public confidence in the capability and will of the monetary authorities." Otmar Emminger, deputy governor of the West German central bank, contends a new system will depend more on events such as progress against inflation than on negotiation of "fixed rules and regulations."

—RICHARD F. JANSSEN

June 1973

Let's All Stop Worrying

THE world's central bankers who met at Basel in early July 1973—and the governments who call the political tune for them—are greatly to be commended. Kipling, who noted the virtue of keeping one's head when all about are losing theirs, would have approved vastly. Faced with a dollar plummeting on world exchanges, forecasts of doom and disaster on all sides and a tempting array of suggestions for action, the bankers latched nicely on what proved in the short term to be the right response and what will basically prove to be the right action in the coming years it will take the world money system to sort itself out. They did, essentially, nothing.

Putting the most positive construction on that nothing, they reminded the world by reissuing a four-month-old communique that they could still intervene on exchange markets. This, as dollar recovery set in on the following days, they proceeded to do, apparently reflecting the Bank of England's sensibly expressed view of its own role in sterling's float. That is, " . . . not to oppose any well-defined trend, but merely to smooth excessive fluctuations." Whether it was this or common sense which steadied the markets following the meeting would be difficult to argue; mass psychoanalysis of foreign exchange traders lies well outside a journalist's field of competence.

But when you consider the many nonsensical actions which were being urged on the bankers—to close the exchanges, to refloat the mark or the Danish kroner, to set a new price for gold, etc., one has to agree with their choice of nothing. Moreover, doing nothing was the only possible choice. Because faced with the present monetary situation, there isn't any quick mechanical magic which governments can perform to relieve monetary uncertainty. Its causes are basic and they are going to be with us for a long while, whatever prices governments attempt to set for gold or each others' currencies and whatever rules they try to make for trading in foreign exchange.

The well-known basic causes of monetary unrest are the long-standing U.S. balance of payments deficit, the resulting $87 billion floating around the world and the communications explosion which moves them about. This last includes not only telecommunications but the growth of international banking, commerce, travel and tourism which can shift vast sums in and out of currencies at the touch of a Telex key.

But what of the doom and disaster, the drying up of international trade and investment which the resulting monetary "chaos" is supposed to cause? Many smart businessmen, bankers and economists are still warning that it could be on the way. Admittedly, it isn't hard to construct a frightening scenario of money chaos followed by shrivelling trade and world recession. But it's the picture doomsayers have been painting for two years. And not only have their fears failed to materialize, but world trade and investment have actually boomed.

Almost two years ago, about four months after Germany first floated the Deutschemark in May 1971, this reporter made a trip to Hamburg to see how German exporters and importers were getting on. The picture was dark. Horror tales abounded. Deals were falling through. Trade couldn't go on like this. Something had to be done. But the success of German trade over the last two years (first quarter 1973 volume $32.2 billion, up 24% from the first quarter of 1971) suggests that the country which has borne the worst brunt of floating and uncertainty has managed to handle it rather well.

And so have others whose business is broadly international. "We've come to look on monetary upheavals as just another source of business expense, like uncertain transport" or fire risk, says John N. Sprague, vice president and treasurer of Singer Co., a $2.3 billion multinational with operations in more than 100 different countries.

Says John C. Haley, managing director of Orion Bank Ltd., a London-based international consortium bank with parents, including Chase Manhattan, in six nations: "We don't think floating rates or currency crises have disrupted trade. And we wouldn't say there's any hesitation in investment. It may be changing direction, but it isn't slackening."

This isn't to say that business has stopped worrying about monetary problems. Far from it. "This is a year of paradox," frets Walther Kniep, executive vice-president and head of European operations for CPC International Inc., the $1.5 billion multinational food company. "Trade and investment should have slowed much more than we observe. We think the monetary upheavals will have a slowdown effect. As a result, we're holding off our investments as long as we possibly can. If a lot of people are holding back like we are, you would think it would have a cumulative slow-down effect. But it doesn't seem to." And business is so good, Mr. Kniep concedes, that CPC Europe is forced to go ahead with its own investment program anyway. "As for our suppliers, like the German chemical companies, there's no slow-

down at all. They're coming out of a slump and thinking again about investing in the States," says Mr.
Kniep.

All of which begs the question of whether the
"chaos" said to be reigning under the "disarray" of the
presently shattered system is really so pernicious. Is it
the "system" or lack of it that's really at fault, and if so,
how should it be reformed?

Of course nobody likes the present uncertainty. If
trade is booming, stable exchange rates could only
make it better. But it's well to remember that floating
has been adopted not because governments particularly
prefer it, but because it has proven impossible, given
world liquidity and communications, to maintain fixed
rates.

Given that the American deficit is the basic problem, it seems reasonable to suggest that the best *monetary* attack on it is to let the dollar rate float down as
low as the market must take it to reverse the payments
flow. If a sharply devalued dollar is painful to Americans, as it will be both in terms of diminished world influence and higher import prices, we have only our-
selves to blame for years of voting down sound dollar
policies. Living off domestic and international deficits
was nice while it lasted but the piper must be paid.

The consequences of those years of deficit and
growing liquidity were long suppressed by the Bretton
Woods fixed rate system. The pent-up forces now un-
leashed are too big to be squeezed back into some unrealistic shape by international monetary mechanics.
But that doesn't mean that the system in its new shape
can't properly transmit the economic forces that will
correct the U.S. payments problem.

It seems, in fact, to be working rather well. Put another way, now that the fixed rate obsession has been
overwhelmed and swept aside, the system seems to be

working *at last*. A country that runs a deficit as large and as persistent as the U.S., after all, is supposed to see its currency devalued. We are seeing it. That, in turn, is supposed to turn trade and investment toward the devaluing country. Fingers crossed, we are seeing that, too. First quarter 1973 U.S. trade figures showed a big improvement with the first surplus in April in 18 months. They'll probably turn bad again before they get better because devaluations always have an adverse initial effect before an upturn. But markets are supposed to understand that sort of thing by now.

Even more significant for the U.S. deficit, in which capital flows have historically played a larger role than trade, we are seeing a rush of foreign direct investment into America. The first signs appeared over a year ago. But the pace has picked up significantly in the first half of 1973 with companies like St. Gobain-Pont-a-Mousson, British American Tobacco, Chloride Group and Nestle rushing in to grab up the devalued goodies.

Remember, too, that these corrective movements are being expressed by investment and trade that was supposed to have dried up in the crash of the old monetary system. For here one seed of the system's collapse, the communications explosion, has also proved a means of salvation. The clue was there two years ago in a Hamburg trader's tale of how a sale of German tires to a Kuwait importer had almost fallen through over uncertainties in the mark's exchange rate. The Arabs wanted to pay in sterling while the Germans wanted marks. But after a little searching around with his Telex machine, the Hamburg trader found an Asian exporter willing to send him raw rubber for the Kuwaiti's sterling which need only be switched by Telex from Kuwait to Singapore. And so the deal, or both deals, were done.

At the time it seemed like an example of regression to barter. But what it also showed, in hindsight, was the fantastic flexibility of international banking and trade, linked by telecommunications, in overcoming foreign exchange problems. Orion Bank's Mr. Haley for example, notes that as a result of the currency crises, "the Eurodollar bond market is dead. But Deutschemark bonds are doing fine. And medium term bank financing has pretty well taken up the slack in the bond market." Thus the very ability of trade and investment to work around foreign exchange problems, to put money where exchange rate set by a free market suggest it will go farthest, should in itself stabilize the market if traders can count on these forces being allowed to play their part.

Thus the inability of finance ministers and central bankers to agree in the last two years on a new system is neither a bad thing nor a good thing. It merely shows they can't impose a system on forces beyond their control. The more sensible approach is to accept the system which has been imposed by circumstances and see that it isn't hampered in carrying out the reforms of the market.

A free market float needn't be so frightening. As Pierre-Paul Schweitzer, retiring managing director of the International Monetary Fund, told a United Nations group during the latest dollar crisis: "Exchange rates . . . take time to have their effects on the underlying payments position and delays in the process are sometimes mistaken for failures in the mechanism. Thus we may witness speculative flurries which are hard to understand in terms of basic competitive relationship. . . . So long as countries pursue sensible policies, both domestically and in exchange markets, these flurries should eventually subside."

As for manipulating the system, central bankers and politicians who really haven't any choice in the matter, anyway, should carry on as before—doing nothing. Rather than be distracted by tempting mechanical palliatives, they should turn their attention to building the political will for the war on inflation in their various countries, the United States most of all. When that and the dollar deficit are in hand, whatever monetary system happens to be in place at the time is going to look pretty good.

—NEIL ULMAN

July 1973

Commentary: Readings 11-15
The Nairobi Agre ment—Continue the Float

Preceding the meetıng of the International Monetary Fund set for Nairobi in September 1973, it was expected that a better solution to the problems of the world monetary system would be proposed to replace the current system of floating rates that emerged from the February 1973 monetary crisis. In advance of the meeting of the IMF membership, a group of financial officers known as the Committee of 20 worked to come up with a proposal for action at the meeting.

However, as September drew nearer, it became more apparent that the Committee of 20 was still in disagreement on some key issues and would not be able to present a proposal for a formal vote. Thus, when the IMF met at Nairobi, no "earth-shattering" action took place to revise the monetary system and the "temporary" floating system was given a greater degree of permanence by its being continued.

At the Nairobi meeting some new, factors did emerge as significant to any new proposal to solve the world's monetary problems and these factors continue to occupy a position of prominence in world monetary affairs today. These factors include the role and importance of SDRs, the exchange adjustment process, the relationship between SDRs and economic aid, the convertibility of currencies into gold and the new multicurrencies.

Readings 11-15 focus on the Nairobi IMF meetings and the events and developments related to them. Reading 14 concerns the IMF's inability to come to an agreement on a revised monetary system at Nairobi and presents some of the reasons for this as well as expectations and anticipations of when these revisions might be decided upon. Reading 11 analyzes the critical situation of the IMF as the meeting opened and its role in progress toward a new system. The powerful negotiations that occurred prior to and during the meeting and the newly significant issues such as SDRs, the adjustment process, gold, economic aid and multicurrencies are all presented and explained in other readings. These issues are especially relevant to any future revisions in the world monetary system and some essentially had their debut at Nairobi.

Thus the "Nairobi Agreement" which many expected to develop and to join the ranks of the Bretton Woods and Smithsonian agreements as milestones in the progress of the world monetary system never really developed. The general concensus at Nairobi was to continue the float. That alone was the Nairobi agreement.

Monetary Muddle

IMAGINE the United Nations facing this situation:

All nations are ignoring the basic rules of the UN charter as archaic tenets of a bygone era. The UN's chief executive has been forced to resign, and his replacement, recruited after a long and embarrassing search, is a little-known professor. UN officials suspect the U.S. is trying to undermine the organization's strength. In all, the future of the UN as an effective tool of international cooperation is very much in doubt.

Fortunately, the UN isn't in such a mess. But the "United Nations" of the world of money is. As officials from 126 member countries gather in Nairobi, Kenya, for the September 1973 annual meeting of the International Monetary Fund, the 29-year-old guardian of world currency values finds itself in an awkward position: custodian of a collapsed monetary order, spectator at a new rule-free currency game beyond its control and expectant godfather to a new monetary system not yet born.

"We are living in a period of trouble and transition," concedes a top official of the IMF.

The trouble, of course, is that the old international monetary system, born with the IMF at a 1944 conference at Bretton Woods, N.H., collapsed in stages between August 1971 and March 1973 under the pressure of massive outflows of dollars from the U.S. and orgies of speculation on world currency markets.

The transition from the old Bretton Woods system of fixed currency values currently features an interim arrangement of "floating" exchange rates determined largely by market forces—a situation that mocks all the IMF rules requiring governments to maintain firmly set currency values. The key question is where this transition will lead: negotiations to restructure the monetary system have been under way for nearly a year, but the outline of the new order and the IMF"s future role are far from determined.

At the 1973 meeting, further discussions in Nairobi probably will clarify the main outlines of a new monetary system, but authorities agree that a detailed plan won't be ready for IMF approval before the 1974 meeting.

The specific monetary issues are deeply complex and shrouded in the jargon of the specialists. Basically, the negotiators are trying to construct a new system that would require each nation to keep its international inflow and outflow of money in reasonable balance, that would permit changes in any nation's currency value to be made without triggering a crisis and that would generally promote the free flow of investment, trade and development aid among nations.

But those easily stated goals can be reached only through marvelously complex means, and that's what the negotiations are all about. Whatever the final form of the monetary agreement, its ultimate success will depend on how well the IMF, as the policeman enforcing the new monetary rules, can make it work.

The survival of the Washington-based organization as an international lender to financially distressed nations and a center for international monetary deliberations isn't in doubt. But the IMF"s future authority, structure and ultimate influence may strengthen or weaken with the changes in the monetary rules.

Some IMF officials fear the overhaul of the currency rules, if lacking enough enforcement authority, could fatally weaken the fund. "The danger of throwing the baby out with the bath water is very considerable," one official says.

And Pierre-Paul Schweitzer, the Frenchman who in August 1973 gave up the IMF helm after 10 years as its managing director, warned that any protracted "delay in restoring an agreed system could erode the legal and moral power" of the IMF. The breakdown of the Bretton Woods monetary system has already "diminished the influence" of the fund, he added.

The way Mr. Schweitzer lost his job and the difficulty the IMF had in recruiting a replacement also have hurt the organization, insiders contend. In effect, Mr. Schweitzer was "blackballed" by U.S. officials, who declined to support him for a third five-year term; the IMF chief ruffled former Treasury Secretary John Connally's feathers by calling for devaluation of the dollar before the Nixon administration was ready to admit that was necessary.

For months, names of "probable successors" and "leading candidates" for the IMF job floated and sank like the dollar. Among a dozen or more such candidates, at least one or two rejected the job, apparently on grounds that the future of the IMF was uncertain and the attitude of the U.S. unfriendly. On July 31, in an appointment that produced a kind of "Spiro who?" reaction, the IMF finally named its man; H. Johannes Witteveen, a Rotterdam economics professor and former finance minister of the Netherlands.

On appearance, the 52-year-old Mr. Witteveen hardly seems a "take-charge" leader. He is a slight, almost frail-looking man with gray hair and long expressive fingers that sculpt the air as he speaks in a quiet monotone. He presents a gentle, rather stoic image, which may reflect inner qualities of scholarliness and mysticism; he is vice president of an international religious and philosophical movement that seeks to reconcile differences between Christianity and oriental religions.

But associates say his meek appearance may be deceptive. As a former politician and Dutch cabinet member, "he knows what it is to fight battles," says one. "He brings us a nice combination of academics and politics."

While his views on specific monetary issues aren't known, indications are that his general approach will be to stress compromise and accommodation. He's also expected to woo Communist nonmember nations, including the Soviet Union, gradually into the IMF fold.

The new fund chief, a top American official notes, is taking over at the most difficult possible time—when the shape of the future monetary system and the IMF's role in it are still uncertain. "It would be much easier to come in a year from now," after these questions are settled, he says.

IMF officials argue that the monetary overhaul won't succeed unless member nations are willing to give the fund sufficient authority to make all countries observe the rules. "If the fund isn't going to be strong in the future," says one top official, "then in my opinion the reform will have failed."

But most nations, jealous of their sovereignty, don't want the IMF in a position to boss them around. The U.S. is especially leery of granting it much discretionary authority. American officials argue for strong, clear-cut monetary rules but against giving the IMF broad leeway in interpreting them.

The U.S. is wary of too much power at the IMF now that it doesn't run the organization as it once did. In the fund's early years, when the dollar was the world's strongest currency and the American economy stood as a giant among war-battered midgets, the IMF danced to the U.S. tune.

But during the past decade, as the dollar weakened, the U.S. economy was wracked by inflation and as Germany and Japan became financial powerhouses, the IMF has moved out of the shadow of the U.S. Treasury. And as IMF membership grew from its original 45 nations to the present 126, the American voting power was diluted from an initial 38% of the total votes to about 21%. Thus the U.S. can no longer be sure of having its way.

American officials don't want the IMF telling the U.S. government when it should devalue the dollar or take new steps to fight inflation. A too-strong IMF, it's feared, could create severe political troubles for an administration by pressuring it to take unpopular steps.

"There's an argument that says that these monetary problems are so complex and vary so much from country to country that you have to turn it all over to an IMF board to exercise discretionary authority, and the IMF board will decide when a country has to do something," notes Paul A. Volcker, Under Secretary of the Treasury for Monetary Affairs.

"My own view," he adds, "is that if you lean too far in that direction, you are putting an impossible burden on the IMF as an institution, because you are giving it too much discretionary authority in highly charged political issues."

This isn't just an American view, Mr. Volcker contends. "A lot of small countries are just as concerned as we are about giving the IMF too much discretionary authority."

Some IMF officials view the U.S. stance, following the "ouster" of the strong-willed Mr. Schweitzer as evidence that the Americans are out to weaken the organization. "The U.S. wants to leave the least amount of discretionary authority with the fund, but you can't have a strong fund without it," one official argues.

This question is likely to be settled partly in the writing of the new monetary rules and partly in a change in the structure of the fund itself. There's strong sentiment, backed by the U.S. and other major nations, to create a new decision-making body within the fund, made up of top-level political officials of member governments rather than of financial experts.

"Some high-level policy board will be set up," predicts an IMF official. Insiders figure that the new body, probably composed of cabinet-level ministers of key governments, would meet only occasionally to settle the most important issues; more routine matters would be left to the present executive board, which would be somewhat overshadowed.

Whether the new body also would over-shadow the managing director and diminish Mr. Witteveen's authority isn't certain. It's understood he favors the idea but recognizes there's some danger of undercutting his own position.

The main issues in the international monetary negotiations are so complex they've kept the world's experts struggling for a year to find solutions. Here is a brief rundown:

THE ADJUSTMENT PROCESS: Monetary authorities are seeking ways to require nations that run big deficits or surpluses in their international payments to adjust their policies so as to balance their inflow and outflow of funds better. But there's a dispute over whether certain statistical warning signals should almost automatically trigger such corrective actions as a devaluation, as the U.S. wants, or merely call for "consultations" with the IMF, as some Europeans prefer.

EXCHANGE RATES: Fixed currency rates made the old monetary system subject to crisis, but "floating" rates make long-range financial planning difficult. Monetary authorities have agreed to return to "stable but adjustable" par values—a generality not yet backed by a specific scheme. A system of rates somewhat more flexible than the old fixed-rate arrangement is expected.

CONVERTIBILITY: Since Aug. 15, 1971, the U.S. hasn't been willing to exchange gold for dollars. Foreign nations holding billions of dollars want an early return to some form of convertibility. The U.S. agrees that eventually all currencies should be convertible into some kind of monetary assets (not necessarily gold) but isn't ready to assume this obligation for the dollar until the U.S. balance-of-payments situation improves and a new monetary system is put in place.

GOLD AND "PAPER GOLD": Most nations agree that gold should somehow be phased out of the monetary system, because it's a too-scarce, volatile commodity. In its place, the IMF's special drawing rights (SDR), sometimes called "paper gold," would become the chief reserve asset. But negotiators haven't figured out how to accomplish this transition.

THE "LINK": Poor nations want to link future distribution of SDRs by the IMF to development aid, so that less-developed nations would get a more generous share of the SDRs. While some Europeans are sympathetic, the U.S. fears such a plan would undermine confidence in the SDR.

—JAMES P. GANNON

September 1973

Power Struggle in the IMF

IF the poor nations get their wish, the world's next monetary system will bear the name of Nairobi, Kenya, a rapidly modernizing African capital. Although it isn't clear that being the birthplace of the old system brings enduring benefits to Bretton Woods, N.H., the hope is that the prestige of developing countries in general and the tourism appeal of Kenya in particular would be greatly enhanced.

That there will be enough progress here to bear out such hopes remains in deep doubt, however. As several thousand officials gather for the weeklong 1973 annual meeting of the International Monetary Fund and World Bank, the U.S. and other nations remain strangely at odds over major issues.

Strangely, because there is a considerable consensus on the overall doctrines: Exchange rates are to be "stable but adjustable," with provision for floating. The emphasis would be on altering exchange rates when economic conditions change, rather than on clinging proudly to outdated rates. Countries with big surpluses or big deficits in their foreign dealings should come under strong pressure to adjust their economic policies, and the IMF's Special Drawing Rights (SDRs) should become more important.

Yet the IMF''s Committee of Twenty deputies doing

the brunt of the work have quietly slated meetings as far ahead as January 1974. If their efforts permit a top-level breakthrough by spring 1974, they would still "have to go hard, very hard" to finish up by the annual meeting in September 1974 in Washington, says Jeremy Morse, chairman of the deputies. His report to the Nairobi meeting will abound, other insiders say, with admissions that further study is needed on "the technicalities and desirability" of many competing proposals.

What can there be to prevent a "Nairobi system" from springing into place?

A common European suspicion is that the U.S. is stalling. To bolster its negotiating clout and soften up congressional protectionists, continental officials figure, the White House wants to give the floating dollar more time to restore a strong trade surplus. American aides counter that they've gone farther than any other nation in offering a plan for a new system, but this leaves a European negotiator marveling at their "extraordinarily rigid" adherence to its controversial features.

According to a more involved theory, there is deliberate stalling by both the U.S. and France so that Presidents Nixon and Pompidou can stage a splashy summit to break the impasse. The spring 1974 timetable prominently mentioned by officials of both nations would tie in with a review of the IMF's obsolete 1969 gold price pact with South Africa, making 1974 the year for a sharp boost in the official gold price. That could ease the Soviet Union into the new monetary system, instantly giving Russia the wealth for buying equipment to develop its natural gas for export to an energy-hungry West.

While that scenario is too Machiavellian for most monetary experts to accept in full, it does point to the widely-agreed basic problem: Even the most arcane of the rules being drafted have a bearing on vital political interests, both domestic and international, making every nation wary of letting power over such bread-and-butter matters as jobs and profits slip into alien hands. "The only issue in all this is who has the power, who really makes the decisions," confides one monetary expert.

That shows up, for instance, in the seemingly eso-teric argument over "objective indicators," or statistics which would tell the world that a particular country ought to take action to avoid getting too deeply into either the red or the black. The U.S. wants a great deal of weight placed on changes in the total of a nation's re-serves, arguing that they should create "a strong pre-sumption" that action is needed.

This would merely speed the natural course of events, U.S. aides argue, noting that a nation ultimately devalues anyway when its reserves are too low to sup-port its currency any longer, or revalues when reserves are rushing in too rapidly. With a recognized statistical rule in place, there'd be much less likelihood of incon-clusive consultations and much more chance of timely and impartial decisions.

But the "Who decides?" issue lurks below the sur-face, skeptical Europeans say. A surge of currency spec-ulation quite out of line with underlying economic trends could trigger the signal, thus transferring at least part of the decision-making ability from govern-ments to private interests. Worse yet, a foreign govern-ment could easily inspire such a speculative surge. Moreover, Europeans note, statistics on reserves are no-toriously subject to manipulation by the government which issues them.

Behind-the-scenes maneuvering to preserve na-tional prerogatives is also taking place on the issue of "convertibility." This refers mainly to the desire of foreign countries to convert excess dollars into "primary reserves" of gold and SDRs. To avoid being swamped by such demands and once again having to close off convertibility, the U.S. Treasury wants the new rules to "place limits on the right of each country to accumulate primary reserves." But the U.S. would let any nation keep on accumulating dollars if it wishes.

That's only another way of saying, Europeans contend, that the U.S. wants to keep the power to pump out dollars without having to worry about buying back all the excess. So the Europeans generally take a directly opposite approach to convertibility—they want the new rules to prohibit any foreign country from accumulating dollars in its reserves. That would leave them free to pile up surpluses in the form of primary assets, while hobbling the dollar and the U.S.

If the rifts were all purely U.S. versus "Europe," compromises might be easier to reach. But alliances vary from issue to issue. As Treasury Secretary George P. Shultz related prior to the meeting in Washington, "The French, who have generally been described as opposing us, proposed a negative rate of interest on excessively large reserves, which is a severe discipline on surplus countries. . . . We thought the French suggestion was a pretty interesting one and we supported it."

While there are some such unnatural groupings, progress is also being retarded by the rather natural rivalry for influence between the rich nations and the poor nations. The best known issue is that of the "link" between SDRs and foreign aid. The poor, with support from France and many other industrial countries, want some form of extra-generous SDR handouts for themselves, on grounds that they are in the most dire need of the money that SDRs can buy, and the things that money can buy.

American negotiators are so adamant against any

link that the deputies haven't even gotten around to trying to work out any details. There are many reasons for the U.S. opposition, but a fundamental one appears to be retaining power to favor friendly lands with direct foreign aid instead of watching it automatically distributed in the form of SDR's according to some politically neutral formula.

A newer and more shadowy struggle for power between the rich and the poor may be taking shape on the seemingly unrelated subject of "multicurrency intervention." Instead of central banks always using American dollars to conduct currency price-propping operations, they would intervene in markets the way a cluster of European countries have taken to doing—spending French francs to buy German marks, for instance, if it is the rates of those two currencies that are getting out of line.

The Nixon administration has proposed this because, for technical reasons, it would allow the dollar to fluctuate more widely against other currencies than it can when it's always being used to stabilize the rates between others. The plan may have another and unstated merit, however. Participation in this plan probably would be limited to the major industrial nations, while the rest would continue to use the less complicated method of intervention.

Conducting multicurrency intervention is something that obviously takes a lot of consultation, so it would provide a perfect cover for finance ministers of the rich countries to get together behind doors which would be closed to the non-participating poor countries. "It could be a backdoor way of getting something like the Group of Ten together again," observes a European official. That group included the U.S., Japan, Canada and key European countries, but has been left to wither away largely because former Treasury Secretary John Connally felt it was stacked nine-to-one against the U.S.

For all their old complaints, though, officials of industrial countries now find it difficult to suppress their longing for the days when they could meet without having to share every secret with, or explain every technicality to, the Tanzanians and Chileans. If suspicions of this sort spread in the "Third World" of developing countries, yet another snag could emerge.

There wouldn't be any need for such subterfuge if the major nations could work out a "restructuring" of the IMF that would be acceptable to the smaller countries as well. Anything as big as the IMF's 20-member executive board tends to be weak and cumbersome, insiders complain, but ideas for replacing that with a tightly-knit directorate of politically-potent authorities raises the same questions of fading influence for less-favored nations.

Perhaps most worrisome to thoughtful monetary negotiators is whether the rules they are drafting actually will be obeyed by sovereign nations, large or small. Holland's recent revaluation wasn't encouraging, with the European Economic Community managing to excuse the lack of advance notice only on the technical grounds that the Dutch didn't bother to ask the IMF's permission either. And if something like that U.S.-backed "negative interest" penalty on excess reserves were a rule when the U.S. has such a surplus agonizes one expert, "how can we be sure that the Congress would actually pay the money?"

So perhaps it isn't so strange that progress to a new monetary system is stubbornly slow. The name of the new system isn't clear to officials only because the name of the game is clear to them—the struggle for power.

—RICHARD F. JANSSEN

September 1973

Clamoring for Paper Gold

IF the poor countries of the world need more money, which they do, and the rich countries don't feel they can spare much more, which they don't, then why not just print a lot of brand new money and hand it out?

Unreal as this may sound, it is blossoming into a serious question, hotly debated at the annual meetings in Nairobi of the International Monetary Fund and the World Bank. It's an issue that is likely to tangle, and could conceivably block, progress toward reweaving of the world's tattered monetary fabric. And that's so even though the question is largely irrelevant in terms of restructuring the monetary system, a torturous process that directly involves such matters as encouraging stability in currency-exchange rates.

The reason is that the poor or less-developed countries, who have never been given much of a voice in international monetary matters, now find themselves in an unaccustomedly strong bargaining position. Worldwide energy and food shortages and rising commodity prices are building political muscle of these resource-rich nations. And, more to the point, while their voting rights in the IMF are minimal, they do have enough power to veto any revision of the articles of the fund— and a revision will be required to establish a new monetary system.

"If they don't get what they want, they can block

whatever the major powers agree on," says Charles R. Stahl, a Princeton, N.J., economic analyst. "What this means is that the big nations will have to go along with what the small nations want."

And what the small nations want is a link between economic aid to them and the creation of a type of money called special drawing rights, or SDRs. When SDRs are created, the poor countries want a super-generous allocation. This would be a sort of automatic aid, avoiding the hassles and disappointments often involved in getting money from the U.S. or other rich nations or even such multinational financial institutions as the World Bank.

SDRs are a kind of fiat money, sometimes called "paper gold," which can be created by agreement of the member nations of the International Monetary Fund. Essentially, an SDR is a bookkeeping entry on the fund's accounts, an asset for its owner although it is acquired without reciprocal payment of any other kind of money and without a promissory note or collateral. Although SDRs can't be used in market transactions, under criteria set by the fund they can be exchanged for U.S. dollars, German marks, British pounds or other national currencies. And these currencies, of course, can be used to purchase tractors, build irrigation systems or repay debts to other countries. To date, allocation of SDRs has been based on each country's initial contribution to the IMF.

It's clear that SDRs will play a central role in whatever new monetary system is fashioned. For example, the SDR will be the yardstick against which national currencies are valued, instead of against dollars or specified weights of gold. And it is expected that SDRs will become a more important type of reserve asset for the central banks of nations, again reducing the roles of dollars and gold, and will increasingly be used by nations to settle debts with each other that arise through imbalances in payments across their borders.

But this broad agreement leaves many technical questions still unsettled. For instance, how do you value the SDR itself? What interest rates should an SDR pay? These technical issues have been under study and negotiation for some time. But the equally key issue of an SDR link with development aid is just now coming to the fore.

"There has been a kind of acknowledgement throughout that the question of a link exists, but very little hard discussion of it until now," says one source. But in meetings of African, Latin American and Asian countries, the link emerged as central demand.

"Developing countries have had some difficulty in making up their minds about a number of items included in (the revision) package, but one thing they are certain of is that they want more SDRs or at least more of the benefits of the SDR system," says James W. Howe, an economist at the Overseas Development Council, a Washington-based foundation. "Since developing countries' support will be needed in order to ratify the (revised monetary) system, I think one can predict that they won't ratify unless the rich countries yield them some additional benefits from SDRs."

There are two key reasons for this drive to link SDRs and aid. First, official development aid—composed of low-cost loans and grants from rich countries to poor ones—has been lagging behind goals agreed to in the United Nations. Second, the developing countries see the link as a way around what they consider the onerous constraints of direct aid from rich nations.

(The poorer countries, for one thing, would have more of a voice through the IMF in the allocation of assistance, instead of being dependent on the decisions of rich countries. And much direct aid now is tied to purchases from the donor country; a grant of dollars, for example, may not involve a transfer of funds at all but rather credits to purchase equipment from U.S. factories. Such "tied aid" sharply limits the flexibility of financial officials in the developing nations.)

Equally important as the demands of the developing nations is the fact that some industrialized lands apparently are coming to regard an SDR-aid link as acceptable. Australian and French leaders have indicated an acceptance, and the United Kingdom isn't opposed.

"There is growing support for some kind of link," Johannes Witteveen, the new managing director of the International Monetary Fund, said at a Nairobi press conference.

But there are still major holdouts, most notably the United States. And the U.S. with its massive voting power in the fund, also holds a potential veto over any plans for revision. The U.S. opposition is based on the ground that a link would be "tangential" to the major business of revision and would risk weakening the confidence in the SDR.

Like any kind of paper money, an SDR has no intrinsic value. It is only a "good asset" if people and their governments think it is. That is, it is only money if there is confidence that it will be accepted in return for real goods and services or other assets. In the short history of SDRs—first created with a $9.5 billion allocation spread over three years beginning Jan. 1, 1970—that confidence has begun to build. Nations have, in fact, been able to acquire foreign currencies through the fund by using their SDRs.

But the original purpose of creating SDRs was to provide a controlled means of adding or subtracting liquidity in the world's financial system. The fear of some economists—especially U.S. economists—is that burdening SDRs with the additional role of economic aid may lead to excessive liquidity (as nations vote themselves big handouts) and thus weaken confidence in the instrument.

In addition, some opponents of the link fear that it would add to the world's inflationary pressures. Money would be created without a comparable increase in the world's output of goods and services, a situation that would lead to price increases, they say.

Advocates have counterarguments, however. Nations wouldn't recklessly vote big pay outs to themselves, the proponents say, because creation of SDRs would take approval by 85% of the IMF. Thus, the developing countries couldn't create SDRs without the agreement of most other countries.

Which brings up an international financial version of Catch 22. The major nations could agree to the link between SDRs and aid in order to gain the support of the developing nations—but then could refuse to create any new SDRs. Leaders of the poor nations are aware of this possibility, and they say they will seek some assurance that SDRs will actually be created before they agree to back any plans to revise the world's currency system.

—CHARLES N. STABLER

September 1973

A Deadline Delayed

AFTER trekking all the way to their long-antici-pated summit meeting in Kenya, international monetary authorities decided to postpone major decisions on restructuring the world's currency system until summer 1974.

The announcement that the finance ministers and central bankers have decided to set a new deadline of July 31, 1974, on their monetary deliberations served only to emphasize the wide gap still separating negotiators struggling to reshape the monetary scheme.

The International Monetary Fund's Committee of 20, which is in charge of the negotiations, decided against trying any real bargaining on the issues at a meeting on the eve of the annual IMF-World Bank conference opening. Instead, the committee settled only procedural matters, including setting the July 31 target for an agreement on the key issues in the negotiations.

Reflecting the stretch-out of the monetary-overhaul timetable, the IMF's new managing director, H. Johannes Witteveen, told newsmen it is "rather optimistic" to expect that the IMF annual meeting in 1974 would be ready to formally adopt newly negotiated monetary rules. He said "there is still a large distance to be bridged" in the negotiations and suggested that key governments weren't yet ready to compromise their differing views to reach a settlement.

U.S. Treasury Secretary George P. Shultz conceded that the outcome of the top-level discussions were "procedural rather than substantive." But he argued this didn't indicate that key nations lack the will to reach agreement. If there hadn't been sufficient progress in earlier talks and the political will to settle, "people wouldn't have been willing to pin themselves down to a deadline," he told a news conference.

Although a final settlement of the monetary negotiations at this conference hadn't been expected, officials had been shooting for agreement on the "broad outlines" of a new monetary system in time for the Nairobi meeting. That hope was dashed by the Committee of 20's decision to defer debate on the key issues since compromises appeared impossible.

The chairman of the committee, Indonesian Finance Minister Aki Wardhana, is scheduled to report to the conference on the status of the monetary-revision effort. While showing some progress, that report is expected to highlight differences of views as much as any meeting of the monetary minds.

A top American official indicated privately that U.S. authorities aren't really upset that the negotiations haven't produced agreement on a new monetary system. He suggested the U.S. isn't ready yet to settle such questions as when and how the U.S. will again accept an obligation to convert foreign-held dollars into other monetary assets. That's a key demand of foreign nations that were left holding billions of unconvertible dollars when the U.S. stopped exchanging gold for dollars on Aug. 15, 1971.

Similarly, sources said key foreign bargainers aren't yet ready to accept the U.S. proposed formula for pressuring nations that run large imbalances in their international payments to change the values of their currencies or take other corrective actions. They said differences over this "adjustment process" and convertibility were the main stumbling blocks to an agreement.

At his first press conference since taking over the top IMF job, Mr. Witteveen said that despite "present difficulties" in the negotiations, "this reform is needed so much that it will be brought about." He conceded that the old monetary system of fixed currency rates, which collapsed under speculative pressures, had been "too rigid." But, he said, "we have perhaps gone to the other extreme" in the present system of "floating" rates that fluctuate freely with exchange-market forces.

The floating rates, the former Dutch finance minister said, have produced an erosion of confidence and "great nervousness in exchange markets." But he wouldn't speculate when asked if lack of progress on the monetary negotiations here might cause additional speculative fluctuations on money markets.

Mr. Witteveen in his news conference indicated he believes that earlier optimistic predictions about the progress of the monetary talks is at least partly to blame for the sense of disappointment felt at this meeting. He said, "Some going up and down in the mood about this reform is quite natural and perhaps will happen again."

Asked if leading governments lack the "political will" to compromise on a new monetary system, Mr. Witteveen replied that "the governments of the major countries have maintained a certain reserve" on key issues, so "it is perhaps to be expected that it takes some time before countries are really ready to compromise."

In his briefing for reporters, Treasury Secretary Shultz said he hoped that many of the main monetary-revision issues could be settled well before the July 31 deadline, so that there wouldn't have to be any eleventh-hour crisis bargaining. "There is a good deal to build on" in future bargaining sessions, he said.

—James P. Gannon

September 1973

SDRs Are In

IN that great can of worms called international monetary reform there is one key element of harmony—Special Drawing Rights are in.

Not everyone is entirely clear on just what a Special Drawing Right, familiarly called an SDR, really is, but it's widely regarded as a "Good Thing." Delegate after delegate at the annual meeting of the International Monetary Fund, however they may dispute other aspects of restructuring the system of exchanging currencies, has called for SDRs to be a central part of the package.

In their search for certainty in an uncertain world, the negotiators see the SDR as a reliable numeraire, or yardstick, against which currency values can be measured, a replacement for erratic gold and discredited dollars. And, with the aid of some tinkering and polishing, SDRs could serve as a store of value for the central banks of nations, a key reserve asset to supplement or perhaps replace gold and dollars and other foreign exchange.

Such is the rising prestige of the SDR that some negotiators at the IMF meeting in the strikingly modern Kenyatta Conference Center are calling it the touchstone of success in working out other issues of monetary reform. If a widely acceptable SDR can be created, it's argued, then solutions will be easier for issues involving how a nation should support or adjust its currency's value, how nations settle their debts with each other and how large accumulations of dollars or other currencies can be converted into other assets.

"SDRs are becoming a new international money," says Fritz Machlup, an international economics professor from Princeton, N.J., and an enthusiastic backer of the concept. In fact, he sees this new money possibly developing even before agreement on other details of monetary reform is reached.

For example, except where domestic laws might prohibit it, commercial banks could begin right now denominating international loans in SDRs instead of Eurodollars and an international but unofficial SDR market could be born.

So, what is an SDR and what might it become?

SDRs were created after years of deliberation in the International Monetary Fund by an amendment to the articles of this multinational financial institution, adopted Oct. 3, 1969. The agreement created a "special drawing account" separate from the fund's other operations. Member nations that wish to participate—most do—are given rights to draw on this account up to specific limits. The first allocation was a total of SDR 9.5 billion, covering the three years from 1970 through 1973.

The allocations were based on each nation's quota in the fund—the amount of gold and currency it has contributed to the institution. The U.S. got SDR 2.3 billion of the first allocation; Botswana and Lesotho got SDR 1.5 million each.

Its bookkeeping entry in the special account entitles a country to obtain an equivalent amount of foreign currency from other participating countries. The purpose is to help the country meet balance-of-payments problems, when it owes more money abroad than it is taking in from investment or trade. The countries that are required to pay out foreign currencies in return for SDRs are designated by the fund, based on their own balance of payments and reserve positions.

The SDR now is valued in terms of gold, 0.89 of a gram. At the time they were created, this was also the par value of a dollar. Subsequent devaluations of the dollar in terms of gold have, in turn, increased the value of SDRs in terms of dollars. In recent flurries of currency revaluations, a number of nations have begun setting central values of their exchange in terms of SDRs, rather than against the dollar.

The purpose of SDR creation was to provide nations with a deliberate, administratively determined increase in reserves so that they could avoid unwanted monetary measures if they ran into temporary balance-of-payments problems. SDRs are a cushion against such measures as deflation of a domestic economy, erection of import controls or devaluation of a currency.

A nation that acquires SDRs beyond its allocation, by selling foreign currencies to a deficit nation, gets paid interest on them at 1.5% a year. This is well below what it could earn on investments of dollar reserves in U.S. Treasury securities. However, some nations have indicated they like to have a portion of their reserves in SDRs anyhow because, unlike depreciating dollars, their value is guaranteed in terms of gold. Only central banks can hold SDRs.

That's where things stand now but there are changes in the wind.

Most countries, judging from what they are saying here, would like to cut the SDRs' link with gold, where the official price is grossly unrealistic and market prices are subject to sharp fluctuations. Instead, they would value an SDR in terms of other currencies, possibly all currencies of member fund nations or perhaps a "basket" of currencies of major trading nations. In this event, the SDR would represent a composite of other currency prices.

The countries also would like to change the interest rates carried by SDRs to more attractive levels. If the SDR was valued in terms of relatively strong currencies, a so-called "robust SDR," it could carry an interest rate that averaged rates available in the domestic economies of the nations involved, a rate that would be relatively low. If the SDR was denominated in terms of all currencies, then its interest rate presumably would have to be the average of rates paid in all countries. Large computers would be urgently needed.

The goal is to find the narrow line between making the SDRs so attractive in value and yield that central banks will be willing to accept them as reserves but not so extravagantly appealing that the nations would never spend them to acquire other assets.

More controversial is a drive on the part of the less developed nations in the fund to link creation of new SDRs with economic development aid. The purpose would be to give these poorer countries a greater share than they've had in the past of newly created SDRs. The move is strongly opposed by the U.S., not because it opposes aid but because it fears overburdening SDRs with a function for which they weren't designed.

Finally, but not least perplexing, a search is under way for a new, less tongue-twisting name. The term Special Drawing Right was selected out of desperation during the negotiations leading up to its creation: the point was to avoid all kinds of words, such as "credit facility" or "borrowed reserves," which had accumulated emotional connotations during the sometimes difficult negotiations.

According to Jeremy Morse, chairman of the group

of deputies of the Committee of 20, many new names have been suggested, "but there's no winner."

One suggestion is "CRU," which would stand for "Currency Reserve Unit." Another is "ICU," for "International Currency Unit."

Some of the many admirers of the former managing director of the Fund, Pierre-Paul Schweitzer, have suggested calling the units "Schweitzers," to honor the man who headed the fund when they were created. Others, while equally admiring of Mr. Schweitzer, have cautioned that this would make the units sound like a sausage or cheese.

Whatever progress monetary reform is making, it's probably not ready for the final suggestion for a new name. That is "CODPIECE" and it would stand for "Composite Objectively Defined Parity Inter-Relator and Exchange and Currency Evaluator."

—CHARLES N. STABLER

September 1973

Commentary: Readings 16-21
Post-Nairobi Developments and the Oil Crisis

One major item of consensus at the September 1973 IMF meeting in Nairobi was that decisions on new monetary reform would have to be postponed at least until the Summer of 1974. The Committee of 20 continued its efforts toward this goal and planned additional 1974 meetings for January at Rome and in the Spring, to continue to negotiate on the major issues remaining from Nairobi. In the meantime, international monetary affairs grew quiet and the exchange rates continued to float. Few expected any major new developments until Spring or Summer, 1974.

Of course, few also expected the sudden political, military and economic developments in the Middle East in late 1973 and these unexpected events once again unsettled and strained the world monetary system. One of the first effects of the oil cutback and world energy crisis on the international monetary system was the demise of the five-year ban on the sale of gold to the open market by seven major central banks, the "two-tier gold market" agreement. The immediate impact of this development was to lower the market price of gold and to give many nations additional options in their monetary policies. However, the long run effects of this development are yet to be seen. Reading 16 focuses on this event.

The major impact of the oil-energy crisis on the monetary system is discussed in Readings 17 and 18. This is that national economic problems will put additional strains on the floating system in the form of defensive economic moves and controls and also increase the possibility that progress toward greater cooperation and agreement among nations will be set back or destroyed. The immediate effect was downward pressure on certain major currencies and uncertainty about economic future.

Two specific and immediate outcomes of the downward pressure on major currencies were the devaluations of the yen and French franc. The yen was devalued in early January 1974 and this is covered by Reading 19. The French devaluation, significant in that it broke up the "snake" or joint float agreed upon by six major European nations and may spell an end to the creation of a European monetary union. This is discussed in Reading 20.

Another outcome of the oil crisis and resulting devaluations is an increased interest in multi-currency currencies, which is reported on in Reading 21.

So the expected quiet period between Nairobi and the Summer of 1974 became very unsettled by the oil crisis and its impact on the world monetary system. These events leave the monetary system in a difficult and uncertain condition: Weakly floating for now but to where and for how long only time will tell. But in retrospect, it is quite a world away from the certain, formal, fixed rate system which existed up to early 1973.

Ending Two-Tier Gold

THE demise of the 1968 ban on central bank sales of gold to the private market presents the U.S. with a series of tempting options with broad economic, monetary and political implications.

These possibilities opened up following the November 1973 announcement that major central banks had terminated the 5½-year-old "two-tier" gold-market agreement:

—The Treasury is again free to begin selling gold to jewelry-makers, dentists, industrial concerns and other domestic users who have had to rely increasingly on imported gold in recent years.

—If there's any profit motive lurking in bureaucrats' hearts, the government could quickly reap a windfall by selling some of its huge gold hoard on the open market, where prices still are more than double the "official" quote of $42.22 an ounce, despite the tumble they took on the news of the gold scheme's demise.

—The Nixon administration's international monetary negotiators can put their money where their mouth has been: After saying for months that gold should become just another commodity like soybeans or silver, they can convincingly demonstrate that gold won't play a central role in a restructured monetary system by fearlessly selling some.

—It's even possible the government could try to counter the Arab nations' oil squeeze by threatening a retaliatory gold squeeze: Oil-rich Arab nations hold a lot of gold they wouldn't want to see "devalued" by a dumping of U.S. stocks on the market.

U.S. officials who cited these new gold options stressed that the government hasn't decided whether or when to sell any of its stockpile of 273.9 million ounces of gold, valued at $11.56 billion at the official price. At a congressional hearing, Treasury Secretary George Shultz declined to discuss U.S. intentions on gold sales; he said decisions on the matter would be made by a five-man group including Secretary of State Henry Kissinger, White House economist Herbert Stein, presidential assistant Peter Flanigan, Federal Reserve Board Chairman Arthur Burns and himself.

A Treasury official said the 1968 agreement among the central banks of the U.S. and six European nations didn't only ban gold-market trading but also stopped Treasury sales of the metal to domestic users. The Treasury is free to resume such sales, he said, though it hasn't decided whether it will agree to provide gold to any domestic users that may seek to buy.

Asked what other reasons might prompt the U.S. to sell some gold, the official responded: "If you sell now, maybe you will make more (profit) than if you sell later." Another source, however, said he doubted "this government" is much interested in reaping a windfall.

Sources suggested that selling some gold would symbolically support a key U.S. position in the international monetary negotiations: that gold should be phased out of the system in the future, to be replaced by the International Monetary Fund's form of fiat money called Special Drawing Rights, or "paper gold."

The end of the gold-sales ban also gives the U.S. a new weapon to use in speculative crises in foreign-exchange markets. Speculative attacks on the dollar and gold-buying rushes could be deflated in the future by sales from the U.S. stockpile, government sources said.

The most intriguing, though least likely, option is the potential for putting pressure on gold-hoarding Arabs through threatened or actual U.S. sales. One official said the new freedom to sell gold gives the U.S. a new point of leverage on the Arab nations, which have effectively used their oil as a lever on the U.S. But other officials doubted that the gold lever would be effective, or that the U.S. would risk hurting so many others in the gold market in an effort to put pressure on the Arabs.

—JAMES P. GANNON

November 1973

The IMF View

OIL shortages and oil-price surges will worsen inflation, deepen a world-wide economic downturn and produce "staggering" imbalances in international payments in 1974, the head of the 126-nation International Monetary Fund warned.

This "combination of circumstances," predicted H. J. Witteveen, managing director of the IMF, "will place strains on the monetary system far in excess of any that have been experienced" since World War II. Warning that the world risks slipping into a protectionist period such as the 1930s, Mr. Witteveen urged a stronger role for the IMF in coordinating national economic policies.

Apparently losing hope for an overhaul of the world monetary system by the formally set deadline of July 31, 1974, the IMF chief conceded that the current system of floating currency rates must continue indefinitely rather than being dropped for a fixed-parity monetary system.

Mr. Witteveen spoke as negotiations on the overhaul of the monetary system resumed in Rome with a two-day meeting of the deputies of the IMF's Committee of 20, which is overseeing the discussions. That session will lay groundwork for the top-level talks among the world's major finance ministers, who make up the Committee of 20.

Before departing for the ministers' meeting, U.S. Treasury Secretary George P. Shultz said in Washington that the meeting will study the impact of the energy crisis on monetary revision. "We will try to come to grips with the facts and the estimates and then see what should be done," he said.

Mr. Shultz said a major concern of the Rome meeting will be the impact of skyrocketing oil prices on poor nations. The increase in costs of oil imports to less-developed nations, he warned, "may wipe out" the benefits of foreign-aid grants from the richer ones.

IMF Director Witteveen said that "the international monetary system is facing its most difficult period since the 1930s." Higher oil prices "will give a sharp twist to the inflationary spiral" this year, he said, while energy shortages "may accentuate a slowdown in economic activity" around the world. He predicted "1974 will almost certainly be a year of staggering disequilibrium in the global balance of payments" due to massive flows of funds from oil-importing industrial lands to the Arab states and other oil exporters.

The uncertain world economic outlook, Mr. Witteveen indicated, has probably put off the time for overhauling the monetary system. "For the time being it is clear," he said, "that floating must continue." The IMF is committed to reverting to "stable but adjustable" currency values from the present floating system under which exchange-market supply and demand forces set the values of currencies. But some monetary authorities have indicated that the IMF's July 31 deadline for agreeing on a new monetary plan probably can't be met now—a view apparently shared by Mr. Witteveen.

The IMF chief warned against "mutually defeating" nationalistic economic policies, including competitive devaluations and added controls on trade and investment. "Short-run national interests shouldn't be allowed, on grounds of economic sovereignty, to stand in the way of an orderly and constructive process of policy formulation through international collaboration," he asserted.

The IMF should act as a "forum" and "catalyst" for coordination of national economic policies, Mr. Witteveen suggested. Some economic policies designed to meet a nation's domestic needs may have harmful international effects, he noted. The IMF must "consult" with its member nations more promptly and must carry more voice in their policy-making to reconcile conflicting interests of member countries, he said.

Mr. Witteveen also indicated the fund stands ready to help nations cope with financial difficulties posed by spiraling oil-import costs. Some nations may be able to handle their new oil-related balance-of-payments problems by using accumulated surpluses of U.S. dollars, he said. But the IMF also should seek "new methods, including ones using the fund as an intermediary, which would help finance the enormous imbalances which have so suddenly arisen," he added.

The IMF chief specifically noted that poorer nations facing balance-of-payments difficulties should be helped with financial resources of the fund. He disclosed that the IMF is "giving detailed consideration to proposals for a new facility to provide longer-term balance-of-payments finance for developing countries."

January 1974

The Arabs and the System

IF all 20 finance ministers arrive in Rome on time for a meeting in January 1974, they will still be too late. The Arabs have already "reformed" the world's monetary system.

The shock of soaring import bills for oil has almost paralyzed the International Monetary Fund's effort to write new rules for keeping currency values stable—an effort that was intended to be the subject of top-level discussions of the IMF's Committee of 20 in Rome. Instead, sources close to the committee say, committee officials are rapidly coming to realize that the present hodgepodge of floating exchange rates has been handed an indefinite new lease on life.

Even before the top-level ministers open their session, a similar opinion was being expressed by H. J. Witteveen, managing director of the IMF. In a London speech preceding the meeting, he said, "For the time being, it is clear that floating must continue." The IMF's Committee of 20 comprises the major trading nations as well as some representatives of the less developed countries.

Putting aside the complex controversies related to resetting rates doesn't mean that the finance ministers face a slate wiped clean of currency problems, however. On the contrary, they are facing a much more urgent problem: how to prevent the massive hemorrhage of money being paid out for oil from provoking panicky protectionism and thus turning the industrial world's economic slowdown into a deep slump.

Prospects for swift, civic-spirited cooperation even on oil money alone aren't bright, participants caution. The huge oil-for-merchandise pacts being shaped individually by Britain, France, West Germany and others with oil-producing countries show that purely national interests are in the saddle, they say. The U.S. initiatives for a grand conclave of consumer countries further cloud chances for great strides, they add.

"The whole Committee of 20 business as we've come to know it is a dying duck," one insider says. The massive amounts of dollars and other currencies that the Arabs stand to amass could surely swamp any system of fixed exchange rates, experts say. The sudden switch of much less than $1 billion from one country to another can overwhelm governmental efforts to keep a rate steady, they note—and they estimate that the Arabs are apt to earn $50 billion of extra loose cash in 1974 alone.

Clearly, once-optimistic planners say, that means that the ministers will have to shelve the effort to return to the generally fixed rates that prevailed precariously until their collapse in March 1973. That makes it pointless to pursue such once-preoccupying topics, they add, as the U.S.-sought statistical tests and sanctions to assure that countries keep exchange rates in line with the IMF view of what is appropriate.

"July 31 will have to be postponed," a key international official laments. That was the 1974 deadline set for top-level agreement on return to a more disciplined monetary system. What is likely to happen on that date instead is a declaration that governments won't use the continuing floats unfairly, other monetary aides say. In the meantime, one official adds, the meeting here is offering "good practice" in agreeing on relatively minor points such as a uniform value for the IMF's tattered Special Drawing Rights.

"It's all a bit unreal in there," says the deputy of one European nation emerging from discussion preliminary to the meeting of the finance ministers. He says that the oil-monetary situation has largely been either avoided or just not raised yet.

But he points out that what the Arabs do with their huge surpluses is "the $64 question" and is certain to be brought up later by the top finance officials. These ministers, such as U.S. Treasury Secretary George Shultz, are "political animals" who will want to come to grips with the dominant monetary issues, he says.

"For us to talk about such matters as Special Drawing Rights or a currency 'breadbasket' (or pooling proposal) and not face the oil problem would be completely absurd," he admits.

What the ministers face is the situation created by the near-trebling of foreign oil prices since the Arab-Israeli war in October 1973. That situation is basically one in which every industrial nation is faced with greater inflation, slower growth or recession, and disappearance of traditional surpluses from exporting more than its imports.

Surprisingly, monetary men say, the biggest danger in the situation is the one that would be least apparent to the public—the loss of trade, or "current account," surpluses. Typically, they explain, industrial nations such as the U.S. and major European nations strive to maintain a trade surplus so that they can afford to pay out money for foreign investments, aid or military forces. Without a trade surplus to offset deficits for these other purposes, a country's currency value is apt to decline, making necessary imports costlier.

Rather than submit to the loss of such trade surplus,

a London expert worries, governments may fight hard
—and fight dirty—to keep them. The tactics include
subsidizing exports, cracking down on imports by tariff
surcharges and quotas and temporarily maneuvering
their currency rates down to gain a competitive edge in
pricing.

One insider in Rome readily acknowledges that
even a partial switch of Arab funds could prove "enor-
mously disruptive" to the world's monetary system. But
the urgency of the problem doesn't make it any easier to
find a solution, he says.

"We're all still kind of stumbling in the dark," he
says. "No one really knows what the 'answers' are any-
more—or what might happen next" in the closely
linked oil and monetary situation.

The deputies of the Committee of 20, who met in
Rome before the ministers' meeting, are fully aware
that, in the context of a massive change in the world's
financial balance of power, their scheduled discussions
on such arcane questions as the proper valuation of
Special Drawing Rights seems largely irrelevant.

The head of one nation's delegation quickly con-
fessed to being utterly "bored" by the SDR talks that
took up most of one day. And others didn't bother to
disguise their disinterest, scanning the speeches that finance ministers were preparing to deliver when the oil
question is expected to surface eventually to the top of
the agenda.

One proposal, for instance, is for the Arabs to lend
their money to the 126-country IMF in Washington,
which in turn would lend it to suddenly "needy" industrial nations such as the U.S. and Britain. The flow
would make up for their trade deficits. The plan is well-
advanced enough to be nicknamed "the Arab GAB," a
reference to the 1962 General Arrangements to Borrow,

under which the IMF received standby credit from what became the "Group of Ten" key industrial countries.

A similar approach would have the Arabs deposit their money for a long period in the IMF's sister institution, the World Bank, which in turn would lend it for long terms to poor countries that don't produce oil in Africa, Asia and Latin America. The poor-country clientele of the World Bank would welcome the money for development projects such as dams and factories.

Conceivably, the officials meeting in Rome at an imposing marble meeting hall in the architectural style known as "Mussolini modern"—planned by the Italian Fascists in the 1930s though completed after World War II—could indeed select one of the seemingly simple plans to do just that. "I wouldn't lose any sleep over that possibility," however, one participant says. While the principle may well be endorsed, he explains, working out specifics would require a long period of consensus-shaping to resolve differing national interests.

Such solutions are probably too ideal to put into practice quickly and on a grand scale, European diplomats say. The Arabs wouldn't settle for lower interest rates than they can get by shopping around in private financial markets, they believe. And the U.S. Congress might not take kindly to chipping in extra sums to permit lofty enough interest rates to be paid to Arabs by the IMF or the World Bank. Many Arab officials wouldn't want to see control of their funds passed to international organizations that lend money to Israel, in particular, and that they suspect are very vulnerable to U.S. pressure in general, these diplomats say.

There have been a few early encouragements to possible monetary cooperation here, such as Arab willingness to participate in the GAB proposal. "After all, most of the Arab funds are in dollars or sterling," one European participant here says. "It really wouldn't be

in their interests to launch an attack on these currencies."

This well-placed European notes with irony, however, that the Arabs "maybe didn't do their homework"
when they pushed up the price of oil so quickly at such
a high rate. The American dollar has been given a boost
at the expense of pro-Arab European nations, he says,
and even the Netherlands oil refineries are prospering
because of European demand.

The Arabs are most likely to continue placing the
bulk of their incoming cash into the Eurodollar market,
the London-centered network in which dollars on
short-term deposit outside the U.S. are lent to borrowers
around the world. Besides the highest possible interest
rates, the Arabs "still want two things that only the Eurodollar market can offer—liquidity and confidential-
ity," a London-based American banker says. Nor are the
bankers bashful about handling what some consider the
ill-gotten gains of the Arabs. "We're all chasing them,"
one senior banker comments.

The Arabs also like gold, a subject that can zestily
deadlock a monetary meeting in the best of times.
Partly because Arabs are understood to be stocking up
on the precious metal, the London free-market price is
soaring. Recognizing that some European nations want
to settle official debts in gold at a value well above the
official $42.22 price, the IMF managing director, Mr.
Witteveen, warns that "we cannot afford to delay"
much longer a gold-valuation decision—despite strong
U.S. opposition to aggrandizing gold's role.

Some officials and private money men agree that it
may not be all that bad to be without a plan for absorbing the potentially volatile funds held by the Arabs. The
banks busily attracting Arab funds are eager to lend
them out, of course, and any government that wishes
can borrow as much as it needs. The British govern-

ment, for example, is already actively encouraging municipalities and nationalized industries to borrow in the Eurodollar market.

—RICHARD F. JANSSEN
—FELIX KESSLER

January 1974

The Yen Goes Down

BOWING to speculative selling spurred by the oil crisis, Japan devalued its yen 6.7% against the U.S. dollar, January 7, 1974.

In Europe, the move triggered still another spate of dollar buying that propelled the U.S. currency to steep new gains against most other funds, as well.

The more expensive dollar could mean higher price tags, and perhaps stiffer competition, for American goods selling in foreign lands. It also means it could cost less to bring foreign cars, cameras and the like into the U.S., if the currency savings aren't eaten away by inflation. Together, these spell fresh problems for Nixon administration strategists trying to balance the U.S. payments accounts with other lands.

Officially, the U.S. Treasury didn't have any comment on the de facto Japanese devaluation. But one official in Washington privately suggested that foreign exchange markets have overdone the downgrading of other currencies. Speaking of the across-the-board deterioration of other currency values against the dollar, he said: "There is a feeling here that things have gone a little too far too soon."

At the latest currency rates, the dollar's value is less than a couple of percentage points from the level set back in December 1971, when the non-Communist world's money managers decided at the Smithsonian Institution in Washington to devalue the dollar almost 8% to help stem a massive capital outflow from the U.S.

That Smithsonian effort was largely a failure, probably because it didn't go far enough, so the dollar was devalued 10% more in February 1973.

When that effort, too, fell short of the mark, most countries decided in last February and March to give up trying to peg their currencies at some fixed rate against the dollar. Instead, they elected to let market forces, and sometimes heavy government intervention, determine the dollar's value, and the dollar kept on sliding until it hit a low about July 1973.

It was then that speculators suddenly decided that maybe the dollar's selloff had been too steep, what with central-bank intervention and an improved outlook in U.S. payments and trade accounts.

What started as a quiet return to the dollar intensified as Arab states started slowing oil production to win support for their battle against Israel. The dollar buying became a torrent in late December 1973, when the Persian Gulf producers and then most others outside the U.S. decided to sharply increase the price of their crude oil.

The two oil moves slammed Japan hard because it depends on imports for almost all its petroleum. Europe also is heavily reliant on imported oil. Even if Arab oil was restored in full, the increased cost would be a heavy drain on both Japanese and European economies. The U.S., by contrast, depends on imports for only about one-third of its oil supply, and thus would be far less hurt than others by the international oil moves.

To one Washington official, there isn't "alarm" but "there is concern" that currency values may stray too far from the February 1973 fixings because of the energy crisis.

It was against such a backdrop that Japan acted, or rather didn't act as it had in the past.

Japan's central bank, which had paid out about $1.1 billion of U.S. currency from its shrinking reserves over two weeks to hold the dollar for immediate delivery at 280 yen, suddenly withdrew from the market and the dollar jumped to 299 yen.

Before the day ended in Tokyo, officials of both the Bank of Japan and the Finance Ministry had made it clear that 300 yen to the dollar was their new target, and the dollar steadied just a notch under that point.

In trading of currency for future delivery, where the central bank doesn't intervene, the dollar for delivery in six months inched up to 319.25 yen from 318.90.

The new 300-yen rate left the dollar only a shade under the value of 308 yen set in the Smithsonian Agreement. That rate had held until the yen was floated in February 1973 when, under strict Japanese government supervision, the dollar slumped further to 265 yen. The dollar started inching back up on the oil crisis, hitting in mid-November 1973 the 280 figure that has just been abandoned.

To further help the yen, the Japanese Finance Ministry moved to encourage importers to bring in dollars more quickly and moved to slow Japanese spending, especially by tourists, in foreign lands.

The 1973 run on the yen and massive Japanese investments in other countries have drained the equivalent of $6.82 billion from Japan's official reserves of gold, convertible currencies and Special Drawing Rights on the International Monetary Fund. That left the total at the close of 1973 at $12.25 billion.

Though the cheaper yen should make it easier for Japanese manufacturers to sell their wares in other countries, most seemed restrained in assessing the de facto devaluation.

Noboru Yoshii, senior managing director at Sony Corp., said the change wouldn't have any special impact on the electronics company. A spokesman at Toyota Motor Co. said the higher cost of imported materials could offset any sales gains from cheaper prices in other lands.

January 1974

France Floats the Franc

IN a startling reversal of its monetary policies, France said January 19, 1974, its franc will be allowed to float on international markets for at least six months to make French exports more competitive.

The move means the franc is almost certain to fall in value when exchange marts open. The franc's de facto devaluation could stretch to 4% or more.

It could also mean a severe, and perhaps fatal, blow to efforts to construct a European monetary union with currency values that transcend national boundary lines.

The move, moreover, raised the specter that other nations may launch similar currency or trade efforts to give their products a competitive edge for world sales. Japan earlier in January, in effect, devalued its yen 6.7% against the dollar for reasons much like those that prompted the French to act.

What the French did was remove official support from foreign-exchange dealings in francs used in ordinary commerce and trade. Francs used by speculators and tourists have long since been floating.

Even the so-called commercial franc actually had been floating against the U.S. dollar since March 1973. But in this float, it was linked with the currencies of West Germany, the Netherlands, Belgium, Luxembourg and Denmark, all of its Common Market partners and some non-Common Market countries as well.

Participants in this joint float had pledged to intervene on exchange markets, if need be, to hold their currencies within 2¼% of each other. For France, this was a pledge that could have cost dearly in its reserves of gold, convertible currencies and Special Drawing Rights on the International Monetary Fund.

France, of late, has been one of the weak sisters of the joint float. From its high of over 25 cents in July 1973, the French franc had sagged to just over 20 cents on January 18, 1974, far steeper than the descent of the West German mark.

West Germany said it offered $3 billion in credits to help France defend its franc's value. But, in a rare Saturday cabinet meeting, France elected to forgo the struggle. The erstwhile prime mover for fixed exchange rates chose to let the market decide the franc's rate.

Finance Minister Valery Giscard d'Estaing said the earlier inconclusive meeting of finance ministers under the aegis of the International Monetary Fund showed there wasn't any "prospect in the near future of international monetary reform."

As with most recent international economic decisions, oil figured high in the French move. Increases in crude oil prices in the Middle East and elsewhere in 1974 will add $5 billion to $6 billion to France's import bill, more than enough to plunge it into a deficit in its international trade account.

A cheaper franc will help France bring its trade accounts more closely into balance because it will lower the selling prices of French goods in foreign lands. Moreover, since Frenchmen will have to pay more of their cheaper francs for imports, an effective devaluation will discourage imports.

Such tactics could prove to no avail, however, if

other countries make similar efforts to insulate their economies from the woes of the world, as Japan has already done before France acted.

The French action, ironically, came only a day after the IMF's Committee of 20 in Rome, after failing to adopt a unified policy on coping with skyrocketing oil prices, declared that "countries mustn't adopt policies which merely aggravate the problems of other countries."

One European monetary official, who earlier in Rome appeared optimistic that Western nations would manage to cope successfully with the oil-payments problems, voiced "general alarm that this is the first of the competitive devaluations." He somewhat tempered his concern, though, with the expectation that France would engage in "a skillfully managed float" to prevent the commercial franc from drifting very far. Inflation is France's biggest domestic problem, he observed, and a much-devalued franc would only add to this aggravation by raising the cost of imports.

In West Germany, the French float was deplored as a "grave setback for European integration," as one spokesman for industry put it. To Otmar Emminger, vice president of the West German central bank, it was "regrettable but understandable."

The French float provided a stark contrast to the Committee of 20's communique, which attempted to paper over an obvious failure to come to any broad agreement on oil policy and major monetary problems though recognizing that large payments deficits would occur.

January 1974

Currency Cocktails

ONCE again it's a busy time on world currency markets. The dollar is adrift in all directions. The long-strong German mark is down. The battered British pound is picking up.

Even the Eurco is down.

The *what?*

That's right, the Eurco. Because monetary crises have been erupting frequently and because finance ministers have made little progress in dealing with them, bankers have tried to work out their own stopgap solutions to the problem of currency fluctuations.

So the bankers invented "currency cocktails" or "currency baskets"—the best-known of which is the Eurco.

These monetary concoctions sound forbiddingly complicated but basically are simple. They consist of varying amounts of currencies already in existence; their paramount purpose is to reduce the risks for businessmen on both sides of a transaction by spreading that risk among several currencies.

The Eurco's value, then, is measured by the value of those currencies on a given day. A Eurco holder, getting paid off, would receive certain quantities of German marks, Italian lire, British pounds and so forth.

In other words, don't expect to see any Eurco notes.

"It isn't a new currency; it's a unit of account," Roger Pitt of Barclays Bank Ltd., in London, emphasizes. Indeed, the bankers are quick to say that they aren't trying to create a new currency; that would run smack into the nationalistic sensitivities of the Common Market governments and into the Market's eventual plans for a common currency.

But the Eurco nevertheless has been publicized; its value is calculated each day by the Luxembourg Stock Exchange and published in the International Herald Tribune and other European newspapers. (For instance, its value January 11, 1974, was $1.13592, or 3.14188 marks, or 0.50524 British pound, and so on.)

The real importance of the currency cocktails, money men say, is that they offer experience possibly leading to new common currencies and to new ways of conducting international transactions.

"I think it's unlikely that the governments concerned would use a commercially promoted currency," says David Ashby, economist for the London branch of Bankers Trust Co. But he sees trends in motion that could lead to "replacing national currencies for all international transactions." That would include transactions among central banks and even traveler's checks.

There is nothing new about using mixed currencies in trade transactions or big financings. Multiple-currency clauses have long been used in international contracts. The problem has been to devise mixed-currency units that favored neither buyer nor seller and that were stable and easy to use.

The Eurco seeks to reduce risk by using proportions of the various currencies reflecting national size and influence (as measured primarily by gross national product). By one recent calculation, for instance, German marks account for the biggest part of the package, 28.77%, and Irish pounds the smallest, 0.97%.

Thus, when individual currencies are devalued or revalued upward or if they float up and down, the Eurco holder suffers minimal fluctuation compared with the holder concentrated in one or another of the individual currencies.

Of course, the bankers and financiers who devised the Eurco weren't primarily concerned about doing a favor for the international monetary system. They wanted to sell their services; drastic fluctuations of major currencies on monetary markets, and particularly the dollar, had made it increasingly difficult to arrange long- or medium-term financings. Thus, the Eurco, a European unit, was created about a year ago after the dollar, the previously dominant international currency, had been twice devalued.

"People started to worry about the dollar," says John Silcock of N. M. Rothschilds & Sons Ltd., the merchant bankers who originated the Eurco. The bankers also were concerned about government heads and central bankers who decreed devaluations and upward revaluations.

"We felt there was a community of interest between European borrowers and lenders," Mr. Silcock says. Eurco backers, he says, were interested in "stability rather than speculation."

The primary objective was to invent a unit for long-term financings like bond issues; the first Eurco bond issue, for 30 million Eurcos, came from the European Investment Bank.

This is the development bank for the Common Market, and as such, its issues enjoy special guarantees from the European community. The bank's sponsorship put some kind of imprimatur on the fledgling Eurco. The first issue was fully subscribed and some private borrowings followed.

The chief strength of the Eurco at that time was its

European character; that's because the dollar was falling compared with the major European currencies. Now
that former strength is proving to be its Achilles' heel;
that's because the dollar has revived.

"People in the market now are critical of the
Eurco," says Mr. Ashby of Bankers Trust. The Eurco, at
$1.13 on the Luxembourg Stock Exchange measure-
ment in January 1974 was between $1.25 and $1.30 for a
number of preceding months. That is enough to take
the bloom off the Eurco.

"People want a thing with a dollar in it," one
banker says. To the rescue has come Barclays Bank,
with its "B-unit." Like the Eurco, the B-unit is a package of currencies, but it uses a different combination.

Whereas the Eurco includes proportions of currencies chiefly according to the size of the gross national
product, the B-unit proposes to use five major trading
currencies—the dollar, the German mark, the French
and Swiss francs, and the British pound—in equal proportions.

If the B-unit currencies had been calculated in
terms of gross national product, the dollar would have
accounted for 68% of its value, automatically making
the unit a dollar-dominated one and losing the advantage of spreading the risk.

The Barclays people are convinced that they can
achieve a "satisfactory spread of risk" and at the same
time offer simplicity, Mr. Pitt says. Barclays researchers
have tested this by running checks on international
contracts between 1967 and 1973, calculating the relative gains or losses of using major currencies or theoretical B-units.

For the B-unit people, simplicity is important.
Whereas the Eurco was intended chiefly for big financings and for the sophisticated financial community, the

B-unit is designed also for use in international trade and contracts.

"This is a practical, fairly low-profile solution to these problems," Mr. Pitt says. Giles Davison, a Barclays colleague, adds that the B-unit's simplicity is a "marketing advantage."

"It is likely to be most attractive for long-term contracts," he says—deals like construction of refineries or the purchase of iron ore or ships.

There are problems, however. The B-unit, like the Eurco, is likely to face skeptical scrutiny from customs men and other officials when it starts to move in commerce. "They'll say, 'What the hell is this?' " an official at one bank acknowledges.

And Mr. Ashby of Bankers Trust pinpoints major problems for borrowers in basket currencies. When the time for repayment comes, they are going to have to muster quantities of various currencies at varying interest rates.

"There is a multiple calculation," Mr. Ashby says. "They never really know what the cost of repaying is going to be."

—BOWEN NORTHRUP

January 1974

Part II

Monetary Crises, Causes
and Effects

Commentary: Readings 22-29

The Problems That Remain

Although the articles in Part I concentrated on the major events and developments in the 1973 world monetary crisis, some of the underlying causes and resulting effects of the crisis were also presented. However, these topics are the main focus of the articles in Part II.

The first articles (Readings 22-24) concern two factors which played a very important role in the 1973 monetary crisis: Gold and the multinational corporations. Reading 22 presents a short history of the relationship between gold and monetary affairs and analyzes the recent interest in gold as part of the 1973 crisis. It should be noted that this article was written prior to the demise of the "two-tier gold market" in late 1973 (covered in Reading 16) and that it may be read in conjunction with Reading 7 in Part I. Readings 23 and 24 concern what may be the most controversial subject in international business today, the multinational corporation. Many criticisms have been directed against these corporations and these articles present both sides of the charge that their currency operations are to blame in recent monetary crises. Reading 24 is especially important in this controversy in that it describes and analyzes hedging operations and activities on the forward exchange markets.

Some of the major consequences of monetary crises and effects of devaluations are presented and discussed in the remaining articles. Readings 25 and 26 raise some serious questions about whether or not devaluations are really beneficial to national economies, with particular reference to the American economy, from the standpoint of inflation and trade balances. Readings 27 though 29 specifically deal with some of the effects of the 1973 monetary crisis on the United States economy.

Although the actual effect of this crisis won't be known for some time, some immediate impacts on stock exchanges, balance of payments and exports are noted and discussed.

These, then, are some of the major causes and consequences of international currency and monetary crises that are discussed and analyzed in the articles in Part II.

A New Aura for Gold

BEAUTIFUL but dangerous. Known associate of Arab sheikhs, Swiss bankers, Soviet commissars, Indian smugglers and black African underground operatives. Possible mystic appeal for American middle class. Reputation for steadfastness but can be fickle. Proven capability for causing dissension among Western allies. Has spent much time in top-security Manhattan jail cell.

The name is gold, and the game of gold is being played for higher stakes than ever before.

Clearly, gold is on the "most wanted" list of many individuals and industrial users around the world; they bid up its price in mid-1973 to about $118 a troy ounce from as low as $44 early in 1972 and from only about $65 at year-end. And the price could go even higher if Congress decides to reopen the potentially vast U.S. market for free private ownership—a right that was taken away from Americans in 1934.

The revival of interest in the ancient metal is a blessing to some. These include European bankers and other dealers; shareholders in South African, Canadian and U.S. mines as well as at least some workers sweating in the mines' deep shafts; and the Soviet Union which mines gold in large quantities and can spend it to buy grain.

But it is more of a curse to many others. These include June graduates who can't afford to buy class rings; Asian peasant hoarders who have been priced out of the market by Western "investors"; and—most importantly—Nixon administration negotiators who find it placing a stubborn new stumbling block between them and a smoothly functioning world monetary system.

All this furor over gold isn't exactly new. Known and fought over since prehistoric times, gold was one of the first metals used by man; the earliest known fine goldwork dates perhaps as far back as 3,000 B.C. As currency, gold has been used since the eighth century B.C., when King Midas (not the one of Greek legends) minted the first coins in Lydia. At times, magical efficacy has been attributed to it, and in the Middle Ages, alchemists sought to transmute base metals to gold. In later years, man no longer thought of gold as the magic metal, but gold still helped make the world go round as the quest for it led to European explorations and conquests in the Western Hemisphere.

These days gold seems to have regained its magical quality. Since the metal has been with us for a while, why do we now have this new golden era? Why has the free-market price nearly doubled since the end of 1972? There are two reasons.

The first is a law as old as gold itself—the law of supply and demand. There has been a steady increase in industrial and other demand for the metal in recent years. Gold is used in everything from fillings for teeth to heatshields for spacecraft. An official of a Swiss firm that refines precious metals says: "There are many industrial uses of gold that have much room for development and expansion." If so, then gold demand could rise still higher.

While demand has been rising, gold production has been slowly dropping. World output in 1972 fell to 44,-

712,000 troy ounces, according to the U.S. Bureau of Mines. That's off more than 3% from 1971 and down nearly 6% from 1970. A major contributor to this drop is the decline from mines of the free world's two biggest producing nations, South Africa and Canada. (A troy ounce is slightly heavier than a regular ounce.)

The second reason for the gold-price spurt is a crisis of confidence— a simple loss of faith in the ability of governments to control inflation. When that happens, people and institutions prefer to hold something as good as gold instead of paper currencies. It isn't only the dollar that has been clipped by the gold shears; indeed, on today's markets just about all that glitters *is* gold. Even currencies that are strong against the dollar —the Japanese yen, the German mark and the Swiss franc—have depreciated in relation to the free-market price of gold. The value of the Swiss franc, for instance, has fallen by one-third against gold since the beginning of this year. So even the Swiss have been getting out of their highly regarded franc and onto the gold bandwagon.

Take Walter Frey, for instance. He is the central manager for Swiss Bank Corp., the world's largest merchandiser of gold. Recently, for the first time in his 37 years with the bank, Mr. Frey purchased a little gold for himself. "It's a good investment," he says matter-of-factly.

In Zurich, Swiss Bank and two other major institutions—Union Bank of Switzerland and Swiss Credit Bank—operate a pool to merchandise gold. There you can find the metal sold across counters as casually as are potatoes in a supermarket. You can buy gold in any size from postage-stamp bars to 400-ounce bricks.

Onto this scene has come a new breed of gold buyer —the investor. Unlike the speculator —who is still very much a factor in the recent price spurts—he isn't in and out of the market with each price swing. Unlike the hoarder, he isn't holding gold for indefinite possession.

The investor is the man with money who has grown disenchanted with paper currencies. He wants not only to protect his capital but also to make a few francs, marks or dollars in the process. So he buys gold bars, usually in a paper transaction that leaves the metal in the vaults of banks for safekeeping. He probably will get out of gold as soon as his confidence in currencies is restored. But that may take a little time. Meanwhile, a lot of people want gold.

"Demand is coming from all over," says Ernst Bigler, the gold chief at Swiss Credit Bank. "As long as we don't have peace in the money market, demand for gold will remain high."

While all kinds of currency are being converted into gold, the dollar is taking the worst beating. In Johannesburg, J. E. Holloway, South Africa's former ambassador to the U.S. and its delegate to the old Bretton Woods monetary conference, puts it this way to an American:

"Inflation is eating away your dollar. It isn't the price of gold that is rising. It is the dollar that is falling."

Inflation aside, a key and ironic result of the spurt in the price of gold has been to make gold hoarders out of the central banks. The free-market price now is impossibly out of line with the so-called official price of $42.22 an ounce; that is the figure set for buying and selling among central banks. With the free-market price approximately three times that figure, the monetary authorities are extremely reluctant to let any gold slip out of their hands for $42.22. And under a 1968 agreement, the major central banks won't sell any of their gold on the free market.

For decades preceding World War I, gold was the

cornerstone of the international monetary system—the most dependable asset that nations could use to settle debts among themselves. Under a strict gold standard, a nation that ran a deficit in its flow of payments with other countries would have to settle the debt by paying in gold. Because currencies were linked with gold, its national money supply would dwindle, prices would come down, imports would become more costly and exports more competitive, and—presto—the payments deficit would turn into a surplus.

Some analysts strongly believe that things still ought to be done that way. They say the gold standard provided the discipline that kept governments from running chronic deficits or from freely expanding money supplies and thus generating inflation.

But this is a minority view. Most economists and government financial authorities now regard the gold standard as politically unworkable. It does cure such ills as chronic deficits and inflation. But in doing so, it can all but kill the patient with such side effects as unemployment and recession, the majority agrees.

These side effects, intensified by the economic and political turmoil after World War I, battered the gold standard beyond recognition. Frequent efforts were made to reestablish gold as a central part of the international monetary system during the 1920s, but all failed. Instead, the international economic scene was marked by recurrent trade wars, competitive currency devaluations as nations sought to protect their export industries and protectionist trade policies.

In the early 1930s, the Roosevelt administration devalued the dollar by establishing a $35-an-ounce price for gold, which was well above previous price levels. But even this effort to reestablish gold in the central role of the international monetary system failed. No nations, beset as they were by the Depression, were willing to accept the discipline and loss of control of domestic economic policies that the gold standard requires.

Then, in the closing months of World War II, the major nations agreed at Bretton Woods, N.H., on a new system. Supervised by the International Monetary Fund, this system provided that exchange rates for other currencies would be pegged to the dollar. In turn, the dollar, then by far the strongest currency, would be convertible into gold.

By and large, after Bretton Woods, all was fairly quiet on the gold front until 1968. Until then, the price of gold as traded among private buyers and sellers had stayed close to the official price of $35 an ounce. But under pressure of rising demand, gold began to drain heavily out of central banks and into private hands. So in an effort to retain the official price at $35 while stemming the outflow of their gold stocks, monetary authorities of the major trading nations agreed to separate the private and official markets, establishing a two-tier system. The quote for private trading continued to move up, but the U.S. held to the level of $35 an ounce for any transactions that central banks holding dollars wanted to make.

Meanwhile, nervous European governments had been rapidly accumulating excess dollars, and the White House learned that they were preparing to turn them in for so much gold that it would have wiped out the Treasury's gold stock—and then some. To prevent that run on gold, President Nixon slammed closed the "gold window" on a Sunday in August 1971. This action meant that the foreign central banks could no longer go to the Treasury and swap their dollars for gold at the $35 rate—or any other rate, for that matter. Free-market trading continued at whatever price was dictated by supply and demand. This trading applies to jewelers, other industrial users, speculators, hoarders, or anybody else—excepting only transactions among major central banks.

A few months later, in December 1971, the major industrial nations agreed on a fundamental realignment of exchange rates. The key was a devaluation of the U.S. dollar by 8%. Technically, this involved a rise in the price of gold to $38 an ounce from the $35 price, which had prevailed since 1934. Other nations readjusted their rates at the same time, with the strong Japanese yen, for instance, being revalued upward against the dollar by almost 17%.

The moves were designed to improve the U.S. balance of payments. But they didn't work. The deficit persisted as dollars continued to flow out of the U.S. By February of 1973, Washington had announced another 10% devaluation of the dollar, raising the official price of gold to the present $42.22 an ounce. The U.S. gold window, of course, remains tightly closed. A foreign central bank still can't exchange its dollars at the U.S. Treasury for gold. For technical and legal reasons, the dollar's value is still officially specified in terms of a particular quantity of gold, leading to that artificial price of $42.22. But for practical purposes, the dollar's value in terms of other currencies and gold is being set by supply and demand, rather than international accord.

Present uncertainty is increased by the "overhang" of $100 billion in U.S. currency that is in foreign hands. These dollars have been sloshing around world monetary markets, adding to inflation and upsetting currency relationships.

That's where things stand now. As for the future, the role of gold—if any—in a new monetary system is under prolonged and laborious discussions by major nations. The outcome is anything but clear. One thing is certain: Gold is further complicating an already complex situation.

Generally, when the dollar weakens in world markets, the price of gold rises. The results are twofold and contradictory: (1) to strengthen the resolve of the U.S. to diminish the role of gold in any future monetary systems and (2) to strengthen the resolve of governments holding gold—mostly European nations—to bolster gold's role.

In simplest terms, these appear to be the possibilities for gold in a new monetary system:

1. Central banks could end their current agreement under which they deal in gold only with one another and only at official prices. They could then buy and sell gold freely at the market price—a price that presumably would drop because their currently immobilized gold holdings would be added to world supplies. (Today it is estimated that the world's central banks hold more than $43 billion of gold—based on the low official price of $42.22 an ounce.) Under this plan, gold would be treated as a commodity just like any other. This system would appear to be the worst for gold hoarders because the gold price is supposed to decline. But would it really? It is possible that many central banks would prefer to hang on to their gold rather than sell it for paper currencies. At any rate, analysts say there is increasing discussion of this proposal despite years spent by central banks in defending official rates.

2. The monetary price of gold could be raised substantially, with $125 an ounce mentioned by some people. Central bankers would be allowed to sell but not buy gold. This plan, in effect, would set a price ceiling of $125 on free-market gold but wouldn't establish a floor. Thus, there could be sharp declines—a factor that could discourage some hoarders. Ultimately, gold would be phased out of the monetary system. As industrial de-

mand climbed, the free price would rise to the ceiling, and bankers would sell their gold to deplete their stocks. That's the way the script goes, anyway.

3. Or gold's monetary price could be raised substantially, but under this plan, gold would then resume the place that it had under the Bretton Woods agreement. That is, the U.S. would have to sell gold at this higher price any time a holder of dollars asked for it. This plan seems to have the least support in monetary circles.

Actually, many observers believe that all three proposals offer only cosmetic solutions. The real problem revolves around trade, the balance of payments and confidence in currencies, they say. A great deal depends on America's ability to control inflation and restore its payments balance, thus strengthening the dollar and removing gold as an issue. When the dollar is strong, central banks prefer to hold on to it rather than gold. The dollar can be invested in U.S. Treasury securities and thus pay a return. Not so with gold.

Eliminating the gold issue is important for a non-monetary reason, also: The gold issue stirs up suspicion between Americans and Europeans. American officials say privately and heatedly that the main reason the French and some other Europeans want a key role for gold in a new system is that merely talking about this pushes up the price and increases the Europeans' personal fortunes. "All these guys own the stuff themselves," one U.S. official charges.

There is another side of the gold coin, however. European officials express strong doubt about Washington's sincerity in saying it wants to cut the links between gold and the monetary system ("demonetizing" gold is the tongue-twisting phrase for this process). Referring to the 1971 American decision to stop converting dollars for gold, one Continental aide demands: "If the U.S. wants to get rid of gold, why is it that the U.S.

broke an international treaty (the International Monetary Fund charter) to keep all its gold for itself? And why is it that the U.S. still has more gold than any other non-Communist country?"

In addition to U.S.-owned gold, about half the gold owned by non-Communist foreign governments is kept physically in the U.S., in a subbasement of the New York Federal Reserve Bank. And that's where that Manhattan jail cell mentioned earlier comes in. The metal is stacked up in cells of the same sort used in prisons; the same clattering and echoing are heard there as in any jailhouse lockup.

According to the Federal Reserve Bulletin, as of the end of May the U.S. was holding $17.3 billion of gold for other non-Communist countries and organizations, out of their total stock of $31.5 billion. The gold reserves held by the U.S. for itself total $11.6 billion.

The fact that so much gold is held in the U.S. for safekeeping suggests something that nobody likes to talk about. This factor, however, appears to be in the minds of officials of many foreign nations as well as of the U.S.: In a major war, which might destroy or heavily damage normal financial and credit institutions, gold is the one type of money that isn't likely to perish. And in case of a crisis in which the U.S. badly needed oil from Arab nations in the Middle East, a little yellow gold (or maybe a lot) crossing the palms of a few sheikhs might bring forth gushers of black gold.

There are less cataclysmic reasons, of course, for keeping gold in a central place. One is the cost of transporting it from country to country. Another is the vulnerability to hijacking these days of an airliner laden with gold.

So it's a lot more sensible to sentence all that gold to an indefinite term in its New York City "jailhouse."

That way, gold can be transferred from country to country simply by carting it from one nation's cell to another.

August 1973

Creating a Crisis

THEY can, and they do, force unwanted changes in
the various values of national currencies. They
strongly influence interest rates throughout the world.
Through a combination of sophistication and sheer size,
they often manage to evade governmental economic
policies. In fact, in the pantheon of demons plaguing financial markets around the globe, they now have dis-
placed the legendary gnomes of Zurich, the ultrasecre-
tive Swiss bankers, as the chief culprit blamed for recurrent instability and breakdowns.

They are the world's multinational corporations—
the giant firms and banks that operate through subsidi-
aries scattered around the globe. The marketing of their
goods and services, in fact, knows few boundaries. They
deal in nearly all of the world's currencies.

The multinationals are currently the center of a
storm of controversies. Devious political doings, irregu-
lar labor practices, unfair competitive strategies—all
these and more have been alleged as standard practices
of the multinational corporation. But of all the controversies, the most complex concerns the multinationals'
highly mobile money. To wit: It is increasingly argued
that no nation nor any international monetary system
can withstand the multinationals' financial power.

"Much of the funds which flow internationally during (a monetary) crisis doubtlessly is of multinational corporation origin," says a massive study by the U.S. Tariff Commission. The companies don't deny this assertion. But whether they indeed possess the enormous power attributed to them by some of the world's financiers is open to varying opinions.

Nowhere are there more opinions on the subject of multinationals than here in the English capital's financial district, the so-called City of London. Here has traditionally been located the nerve center of what is called the Eurodollar market—that is, dollars on deposit in Europe and therefore beyond the purview of U.S. government control. With the growth of multinationals, this market has vastly diversified to the point that it is more appropriately measured in "Eurocurrency," consisting, say, of Euroyen or Euromarks—a kind of world money that integrates, sometimes to their discomfort, the financial markets of the various nations.

The power to move these deposits among banks in different countries is wielded by a variety of sources, ranging from the central banks of nations to wealthy individuals. But these days, such assets are largely controlled by the multinational banks and corporations. And if the multinationals' power is regarded in some quarters as threatening the world's financial structure, the multinationals themselves, while by no means minimizing their role in world finance, frequently maintain that their monetary maneuvering is purely defensive— an effort, in fact, to play a legitimate business game without being at the mercy of changes in the value of their chips.

"The international treasurer must try to avoid a serious economic book loss to the company in dollar terms on account of even small changes in foreign currency values against the dollar," says William F. Ryan, international finance director of one of the great multinationals, Allied Chemical Corp. "To do so, he plans ahead to keep a balanced position in his financial assets and liabilities overseas. For example, if the deutsche mark is a relatively stronger currency against the dollar and the Italian lira is a relatively weaker currency against the dollar and a change in the mark-lira rate is likely, he would prudently aim to increase his mark financial assets and decrease his mark liabilities, while decreasing his lira assets and increasing his lira liabilities."

But if the rationale is obvious—the multinational company offsets its losses in one currency (translated into dollars) with gains from another—so, too, is the result: The weakness of the currency that is dumped is aggravated, and the strength of the sought-after currency is enhanced. And while international trade has always involved this process, the growth of multinational corporations in recent years—along with improvements in intercontinental communications—has sent the size and speed of capital flows soaring and, critics say, has consequently accelerated the pace of world monetary crises.

In London, Christopher Tugendhat, who represents the City in Parliament (much as if Wall Street had its own Congressman) remarks on a kind of "go-go" fever that has increasingly pervaded the control centers of multinational money management. In a recent book, he points out that when performance-oriented mutual fund managers all follow each other in and out of the same stocks, "upward and downward swings (in prices) are invariably exaggerated." He adds: "In certain circumstances, the same applies to currencies."

True, few deny that sometimes the multinationals enter into monetary maneuvering because they simply can't do otherwise—that there is in actuality much to buttress their claims that their moves are defensive. A New York banker, for example, analyzing the genesis of the 1973 currency crisis (which resulted in the second devaluation of the dollar) says, "Our big customers (multinational corporations) weren't in it at the start, and they held back quite a while; they thought it would blow over. But as it kept building up, they finally had to step in and protect themselves." (This particular protection involved short sales of borrowed dollars and purchases of Swiss francs, German marks and Japanese yen.)

But despite what they say is their avowed dedication to purely defensive money management, the temptation for multinationals to use their financial prowess in speculative ventures is sometimes too great to be suppressed. "Certainly we take uncovered (speculative) positions in currencies," says the representative of a New York bank here in London, "and it can be very profitable."

Considering the size of the multinationals' assets, it isn't surprising that any moves on their part—speculative or otherwise—are greeted with concern, not only in the City and on Wall Street, but in Washington and Whitehall as well. According to the Tariff Commission study, for example, private institutions on the international financial scene controlled some $268 billion in short-term liquid assets at the end of 1971. By comparison, the reserves of the world's major central banks— the foreign exchange holdings that they use to buy or sell currencies to defend against unwanted price changes—come to less than $68 billion. Germany, for example, has about $22 billion in foreign exchange reserves, France has $5 billion, Great Britain $4 billion and Japan $17 billion.

(According to some major banks and corporations, the Tariff Commission figure is unrealistic and thereby distorts the comparison between the wealth of the multinationals and the central banks.) Economists at New

York's First National City Bank, for example, term the commission's estimate for the corporations "naughty numbers" and say it includes about $138 billion in non-liquid assets and double-counting. But even if this figure were to be subtracted, the multinational treasury would still be more than enough to precipitate a crisis in the event of even slight maneuvering. In the currency crisis that led up to the 1973 dollar devaluation, well under $10 billion was sufficient to break down the alignment of exchange rates agreed on 14 months earlier at the Smithsonian Institution and, in fact, to sink the whole monetary system.

Further enhancing the power of the multinationals is the fact that they can bring about major changes in a nation's balance of payments even without outright transfers of funds. The process is familiarly called "leads and lags," and its effect can be devastating. An example: Great Britain in one recent month had export-and-import-payment flows totaling $4.3 billion and a trade deficit of $269 million. If, because of doubts about the pound, British importers hastened payment and exporters respectively delayed collections by 10% —which is well within the realm of possibility—the nation's trade deficit would have widened to $699 million.

A nation can, of course, almost entirely seal its borders against money flows and thereby prevent such swings. The Soviet Union, China and other countries with tight economic controls and currencies that aren't readily convertible are cases in point. But such preventive medicine has its side effects in that investments are blocked and trade is effectively strangled.

How then can national money managers curb speculative, and disruptive, flows of capital while not frightening off wanted investment and trade? In the wake of each recent currency crisis, nations have tried to deal with this dilemma in a variety of ways. France, for example, has a two-tier currency; the price of francs used in trade is supported against some other European currencies, while the price of francs used in internal financial transactions floats in response to market forces. Several other nations now have what might be called negative interest rates on deposits from non-residents in their banks; the nonresident has to pay the bank to withdraw money.

But such controls, money men say, really don't work very well in the long run. "There are too many ways to skin a cat," says a New York foreign exchange dealer. By way of example, he cites the case of a Latin American subsidiary of a large multinational company. The subsidiary was amassing large profits, the dollar value of which was threatened by an almost certain devaluation of the host country's currency. And the country's weak balance of payments, which had precipitated the idea of devaluation, had already caused it to block companies from exporting assets to a safer haven.

The solution: On orders from headquarters, employes throughout the company's worldwide network began to order all their airline tickets through the Latin American subsidiary. This ploy drained away the subsidiary's endangered profits to the tune of about $100,-000 a year and served the dual purpose of trimming expenses for the company's other affiliates.

Indeed, multinationals have proved to be exceedingly versatile at outwitting national economic policies. Take the case of a devaluation stemming from a country's desire to curb inflation. Knowing that companies will often try to circumvent devaluation to maintain profit margins by simply raising prices, the move to devalue a currency is often accompanied by price controls. But a clever multinational management, anticipating devaluation, will prior to the devaluation announce an artificially high price for its products, which it then quietly sells at a discount; when devaluation occurs, the company simply eliminates the discounts, thereby maintaining its profit margin.

"If necessity is the mother of invention, restrictions must certainly be the father of ingenuity," says Yves-Andre Istel of Kuhn, Loeb & Co. And other observers agree that such ingenuity will continue to triumph, since the benefits of trade and investment among nations are generally too desirable for governments to have them institute more restrictive controls.

"Bureaucrats and governments keep trying to control markets, but history proves they can't," asserts Milo Vesel, managing director of the Paris-based international arm of Smith, Barney & Co. He adds: "Thomas Aquinas kept warning the peasants they would go to hell if they raised the price of potatoes. But people took the chance and raised the prices anyhow."

In terms of the Eurodollar market, this situation means that efforts to control the market by one nation or a group of nations would simply drive it elsewhere—to the Bahamas, say, or to Zurich or indeed anywhere it could operate free of control. This eventuality isn't lost on the British, whose authorities reject the idea of regulating the Eurodollar by controlling financial intermediaries in London—even though it was through the Eurodollar market that $3 billion flooded into England in a matter of days in 1972, knocking the pound sterling off its fixed peg and into a float that still continues. The British reasoning, of course, is that any effort to restrict Eurodollar operations would simply deprive London of the business.

(Many nations do control participation by their own residents in the Eurodollar market. But there is no supranational control, and there is little confidence such control could ever come about.)

The British have perhaps learned a lesson from

what some consider to be a U.S. mistake. A recent study
by Rimmer de Vries, international economist of New
York's Morgan Guaranty Trust Co., indicates U.S. efforts to shore up the nation's balance of payments by
restricting financial outflows "are responsible for the
export of the international banking business of U.S.
banks.

"The U.S. is the largest industrial country and has
the most advanced banking system and the best developed money and capital markets in the world and therefore should be a much more important international financial center than it has been," Mr. de Vries says.
"The enormous expansion of international financial activity in the past decade or more has largely bypassed
the U.S. because of restraints and regulations." (One
major result: In order to compete in international markets, U.S. banks have sharply expanded their overseas
operations and created 35,000 jobs in the process, all
outside the U.S.)

In fact, most analysts say the Eurodollar market
has more advantages than disadvantages for the world
monetary structure. "On balance, most observers would
agree that the Eurodollar market has been a major constructive force in the financing of economic growth and
expanded international trade," John J. Balles, president
of the Federal Reserve Bank of San Francisco, said in
an analysis.

One advantage, Eurodollar proponents contend, is
that the market is an increasingly important source of
capital for companies and governments. For example,
the investment banking firm of White, Weld & Co. says
that 1972's new issues of international bonds sold in the
Eurodollar market totaled a record $5.66 billion, some
$2 billion more than in 1971 and more than double the
1970 figure. The bonds were denominated in 10 different currencies and combinations of currencies, with Eu-

rodollars accounting for $3.3 billion. (Affiliates of U.S. companies borrowed $1.8 billion of the total.)

"The record volume of new-issue activity again amply demonstrated the resilience and adaptability of the international bond market," White Weld says.

If the Eurodollar market is here to stay, is there any ready solution to the multinational corporations' potential for transmitting monetary strains from nation to nation? Apparently not. And the reason, some analysts argue, is that the disruptive problem of short-term capital flows brought on by multinational corporate activity is basically a symptom rather than a cause of world monetary malaise.

"Regulation of the Eurodollar market isn't simply a technical matter but is rather an aspect of the broader problem of international monetary cooperation," says an early study of the question by Donald R. Hodgman, a professor of economics at the University of Illinois. "This in turn merges into the still broader issues of international economic and political cooperation."

—CHARLES N. STABLER

April 1973

Covered Cash

L ATELY, Guenter Reineke, manager of banking for Volkswagen Co. of America, has been devoting most of his time to an area that he barely thought about until several years ago—foreign exchange.

The cause of his preoccupation is the steep decline in the value of the U.S. dollar in world monetary markets. As a result, Volkswagen Co., the U.S. unit of Volkswagenwerk A.G., which imports some 500,000 automobiles annually into the U.S., finds itself in the uncomfortable position of having to pay out more and more dollars for the German marks it needs to buy cars from its parent concern.

Although the dollar has dropped more than 30% in value relative to the mark in the first six months of 1973, the swing hasn't proved as costly as it might because of the company's adept use of the massive but little-known "forward market" in foreign currencies. Since 1969, the company has used the market to buy millions of dollars worth of German marks for future delivery against anticipated future car deliveries.

"Without the forward market, we would have to be raising our dealer prices every week, which of course is impossible," Mr. Reineke observes. "It has really saved us."

Mr. Reineke has a lot of company in the forward

market these days. "Until the late 1960s a lot of companies heavily involved in international operations ignored the forward market except during occasional currency crises," says Talat M. Othman, vice president of foreign exchange operations at Harris Trust and Savings Bank of Chicago. "Now, we find that companies are increasingly hedging foreign-exchange exposures in the forward market on a regular basis."

In allowing companies to hedge their currency risks, the forward market performs a broader function: It permits international trade and investment to continue in the face of the sort of rapidly fluctuating exchange rates and stiff controls on international capital movements that now exist.

"Unless businessmen remain able to hedge in the forward market fairly cheaply and easily, we could see a contraction in these areas," says Rimmer de Vries, vice president and chief international economist of Morgan Guaranty Trust Co. in New York. "So far the forward market seems to have weathered the recent upheavals fairly well."

How the forward market works can be illustrated by a hypothetical example. Say a U.S. company contracts to purchase machinery from a German company for delivery six months hence at a set price in marks. The U.S. company could then call a bank and buy the marks for delivery in six months at a dollar price only slightly higher than the current dollar-mark exchange rate. The bank, in turn, would probably buy the marks for six-month delivery from a customer wanting to exchange marks for dollars or from another bank if it didn't have mark balances of its own available.

The U.S. company benefits from the transaction by locking in the cost of the marks it will need regardless of what happens to the dollar-mark exchange rate in the meantime. The bank makes a small profit on the dealer "spread," or the difference between the selling price and what it paid for the currency involved.

No statistics are kept on forward market activity, but experts like Robert Z. Aliber, professor of international finance and economics at the University of Chicago Graduate School of Business, estimate the size of the market at more than $500 billion a year, double the level of a decade ago.

Conducting the trading are several hundred major banks in such world money centers as New York, London, Frankfurt, Zurich, Tokyo and Brussels, which make forward markets as an adjunct to their regular currency-conversion operations.

Behind the surge in forward market activity is the increased risk faced by businesses with international operations of sharp exchange rate shifts between currencies. Since 1971, the U.S. dollar, the linchpin of the world monetary system, has been devalued twice. The latest dollar devaluation in February left the post-World War II monetary order of pegged exchange rates in shambles as most of the world's key currencies were set afloat against the dollar.

A number of U.S. companies have taken large and well-publicized foreign-exchange losses in recent months. Gulf Oil Co., for instance, reduced its 1972 operating earnings by $25 million because of the upward revaluation of its long-term borrowings repayable in German marks and Swiss francs.

The forward market itself hasn't been immune to the recent world monetary turbulence. For one thing, the costs of hedging in the market have risen markedly. These costs reflect both the dealer spread charged by the bank and the spread between the current exchange rate and forward exchange rate of a currency. Since the advent of floating rates, both spreads have widened considerably. For example, the dollar rate for Swiss francs for delivery in six months (a typical forward-contract period) is 5.5% higher on an annual basis than the current spot exchange rate, while in 1972 the spread between the spot and the six-month rate was less than 2% on an annual basis.

Exchange controls have made forward dealing in some currencies more difficult in recent months. Italy doesn't permit its banks to deal in forward lire against the dollar unless invoices are produced to prove that the forward cover is being sought for a commercial transaction. Forward cover in Japanese yen, always difficult to obtain, is even more so now because of tightened restrictions by the Japanese government on domestic and foreign banks operating there, many U.S. corporations complain. "The yen forward market can be characterized in one word—atrocious," says the treasurer of a large U.S. television manufacturer.

Despite such irritants, most U.S. companies say they are doing business as usual overseas, raising prices when they can to offset higher forward-market and other foreign-exchange costs or, in some cases, merely absorbing the additional expenses. "With flexible exchange rates, foreign exchange has become just another cost of doing business overseas," says William Valiant, treasurer of Borg-Warner Corp., a diversified Chicago-based manufacturer.

Hedging isn't the only means companies have of protecting themselves against foreign-exchange losses. Over the years multinational companies have developed elaborate foreign-asset management programs for this purpose, which involve such strategies as switching cash and other current assets into strong currencies while piling up debt and other liabilities in depreciating currencies. Companies also encourage quick payment of bills in weak currency areas by offering sizable discounts while extending lavish credit in strong currency areas.

But, for a sizable number of trade and capital transactions, forward hedging affords the only means of protection. A foray into the forward market by Jewel Cos., a Chicago-based supermarket chain, provides an excellent example of the mechanics of such transactions.

In early 1971, John Balch, Jewel's treasurer, became concerned that a debt of 37 million German marks (then about $10 million) incurred by the company two years earlier might cost Jewel even more in dollars to pay off if the dollar were to weaken. So he bought 37 million marks for delivery in six months through a Chicago bank at close to the then-prevailing exchange rate of 27 cents per mark. As is typical with such transactions, the bank required no dollar cash outlay until maturity of the contract in late August 1971.

By the time the contract came due, the mark had appreciated in value to about 29 cents per mark. Jewel received the difference between the contract price of the marks and their higher current market value, or a profit of $500,000. The company then bought another six-month contract covering the loan. This, upon maturity in February 1972, netted Jewel another $500,000 profit.

As a result of the two forward contracts, Jewel suffered only a small net loss when it paid off the mark loan in early 1972. Despite the fact that the mark had jumped 10% in value relative to the dollar during the life of the loan, the $1 million profit in the forward market offset most of the foreign-exchange loss.

Multinational companies and others also take forward positions in currencies for profit. The attraction of the market for speculators is that it permits them to buy currencies or sell them short without immediate cash payments.

Few companies will discuss their forward speculation because the practice is frowned on by governments and central banks fearful of its potentially disruptive impact on exchange rates. The treasurer of a major conglomerate with world-wide operations says: "If we took speculative positions in the forward market, I'd never admit it, because it's the worst kind of public relations imaginable for getting along with various governments, including our own."

Typical of corporate reticence on the subject is the reaction of a treasurer of a large Midwestern capital-goods company when asked whether his company ever speculated in the forward market. After protesting that his company only took forward positions to hedge currency risks, he bemoaned the fact that he hadn't bought several million dollars worth of yen in the forward market in early 1971 because he "would have made a killing for the company" from the yen's subsequent rise.

Yet speculation abounds, frequently under the guise of hedging. "When a large and valued customer of the bank wants forward cover, we provide it without asking any questions despite the fact that at least some of these positions are probably speculative," says the chief foreign-exchange trader of a large New York bank.

The biggest speculators in the forward market are the banks themselves—especially in Europe, where currency speculation by banks has been traditional. The speculative positions taken by U.S. banks are typically of a short-term, overnight variety. "We'll delay laying off a position in a currency if our information and intuition tell us that the currency is moving in a certain direction," explains a New York bank trader. "These positions can be quite profitable."

U.S. banks limit the size of uncovered currency positions they permit their foreign-exchange desks. For larger banks, these limits rarely exceed $5 million per currency.

However, bank traders have been known to exceed these limits. In one spectacular case in the mid-1960s, a trader in the Brussels branch of First National City Bank of New York lost more than $8 million on a massive position in forward British pounds.

Private citizens wanting to speculate in currencies generally are barred by banks from the forward market, though banks occasionally will make exceptions for individuals with "pull" or very large accounts.

Forward trading is carried on in special foreign-exchange trading rooms where spot and forward transactions are done simultaneously. The trading desks typically have a half-dozen to a dozen traders, each of whom concentrates in trading specific currencies and keeping an up-to-the-minute tally of the bank's overall position in various maturities.

The pressure on traders, particularly recently, is enormous. During world monetary crises some New York banks stay open from 4:00 a.m. to late in the evening. Cacophony reigns as Teletypes with messages from all over the world clatter constantly and telephone calls pour in from customers, overseas branches and New York foreign-exchange brokers, who act as middlemen between U.S. banks. Emotional breakdowns and suicides by traders aren't uncommon during hectic periods.

Millions of dollars of currency are traded in a matter of seconds, normally by Telex. "We prefer trading by Teletype (rather than telephone) because then there can't be any dispute over terms," explains one trader. With the exception of French banks, which insist on using French, foreign exchange trading is done in English.

—JONATHAN R. LAING

July 1973

The Bitter Fruits of Devaluation

INFLATION is plaguing not only the housewife but also the economics profession. Over 1973, wholesale prices rose 18.2% and consumer prices rose at a rate of nearly 9%. Conventional economic views did not predict and cannot explain increases of this magnitude.

The money supply has expanded at a rate some consider too high from a policy perspective, but not one that is terribly high for comparable periods over the past decade. Using past relationships between rates of growth of the money supply and inflation as our guide, it is virtually inconceivable that excessive money growth is to blame for the almost unprecedented rate of inflation recently experienced.

For quite some time now fiscal policy has been if anything contradictory. The full employment budget has been balanced, the actual deficit has shrunk and total outlays have been tightly controlled. Even government purchases, which in real terms soared prior to 1969, have been substantially reduced. All in all fiscal policy does not appear to be the culprit.

Advocates of Phillip's curves, price bulges and a whole host of other views are also faced with an inordinate amount of inflation to explain with inadequate sources. Unemployment is higher than at many times in the recent past, yet inflation is higher than at any time. Even the overall price controls program couldn't have increased inflation this much.

Nor can the recent high rates of inflation in the United States be explained as solely a part of an overall world-wide inflation problem caused by shortages of food and other goods. Over the same period that the rate of inflation in U.S. wholesale prices registered 26.5%, we find the German and British rates at 6.2% and 7.3% respectively. World-wide inflation has been great, but other nations did not experience the sudden burst that struck the U.S.

There is one way, however, to explain a large portion of the sudden burst of price increases in the United States. All economists recognize that the devaluation of the dollar, in December 1971 and again in February 1973, has some inflationary impact. If you view the domestic economy as basically a closed system with a few international inputs, as most economists traditionally have, then you will see this effect as slight. But if you conceive of the U.S. as but a part of a relatively unified world market, the inflationary effect of devaluation must be seen as far more dramatic, indeed fully adequate to explain the kind of inflation the U.S. has recently experienced.

The conventional doctrine relating domestic inflation to currency depreciation is in essence straightforward and simple. When a country devalues, say by 10%, it will now cost $110 to buy the same amount of currency that $100 used to buy. The price of imported goods will automatically rise by the amount of devaluation.

To compute the overall inflationary effect of a devaluation, therefore, one need only know the amount of the devaluation and the share of the total goods bundle imports compose. Of total demand in the United States, imports comprise roughly 5%; therefore, according to the conventional approach, a 10% devaluation of the U.S. dollar should add only 0.5% to the appropriate price index—a trifling amount.

While many versions of the conventional view of the inflationary consequences of a devaluation are far more complicated, the above description captures its essence. It is important to note that this view assumes that the foreign currency price of imported goods does not change—only the domestic currency price changes. The prices of all domestically produced goods are also assumed to remain unchanged.

This conventional approach, however, is not the only view of the consequences of devaluation. The chief alternative sees the world economy not as a collection of loosely related closed systems, but as one relatively efficient market. In an efficient market, the price of goods does not depend on the amount flowing from one geographical sector to another.

To determine, say, how a change in the price of apples in Illinois would affect the price of apples in Kansas, very few economists would study the flow of apples from one state to another. Rather, they would expect that even if the traditional flow of apples was little changed, the price in Kansas would rise to compensate for the higher price in Illinois.

Devaluation is an attempt to change the price of apples and other goods in one nation relative to another, by changing the relationship between the yardsticks by which those prices happen to be measured. If markets are efficient, the real price of apples—relative to cars or hours of labor or other things of value—will not be affected. Nor will this real price be different, other things being equal, in one nation or another. Thus, if the yardsticks change, the prices measured by them will have to change in a way that preserves the original relationship of real prices.

Or consider the same phenomenon from the point of view of one nation. If any country produces goods that it both trades and consumes domestically, then items sold for domestic consumption will not differ in price from items sold for foreign consumption. Likewise, foreign imports into any country should also sell at the same price as domestically produced import substitutes —both before and following a devaluation. If these prices did not adjust in this manner, speculators could make virtually unlimited profits by purchasing goods in one country and selling them in another country.

Various artificial as well as natural barriers, of course, keep any market from being completely efficient, and these may be higher in international markets than in domestic ones of a similar size. But if there ever were any reasons to conceive of international markets as greatly different from domestic ones, they surely have been greatly eroded by the negotiated reduction in trade barriers and improvements in international transportation and communication. The empirical results of devaluations around the world, moreover, are fully consistent with efficiency in international markets.

This alternative view of devaluation predicts, for example, that devaluations do not improve a country's trade balance. Because nominal prices will adjust and real prices will remain unchanged, the devaluing nation will not gain a competitive advantage.

With the available data on the effect of devaluations, in fact, one would be hard pressed to find much of a relationship at all between exchange rate changes and trade balances. This, of course, does not mean that I have proven that a relationship does not exist, only that I have been unable to find one. However, I did find that trade balances appear to be closely related to a country's growth rate relative to other countries. That is, when a country's growth rate increases, its trade balance tends to deteriorate, and contrariwise. This view is entirely consistent with the recent improvement in the U.S. trade balance, coming as it did with the peaking of the U.S. growth rate in 1973.

Similarly, the alternative view predicts that a devaluing nation will suffer rapid inflation relative to the rest of the world. Its nominal price levels will have to increase rapidly to restore the original relationship of real prices with real prices elsewhere in the world. This effect, of course, does not depend on the actual flow of goods from one nation to another. This prediction is also consistent with the U.S. experience with devaluation in the past 30 months or so. Other countries also provide a rich inventory of case studies.

After France's 1958 devaluation, its wholesale price index rose almost 14.5% over the three succeeding years as compared to a rise of 2.4% in Germany, 5% in the United Kingdom, and a fall of 0.1% in the United States. After its 1969 devaluation, France's wholesale price index rose 17% in three years, again more than the contemporaneous U.S., German or British rises. In the three years prior to its devaluation, France had experienced only a 5% increase in its wholesale price index.

Looking at the the United Kingdom experience of 1967, a similar pattern emerges. In the three years before the pound was devalued, Britain's wholesale price rise was 6.2%, while in the three years after the devaluation, the same index rose 16.8%. Equivalent U.S. and German price increases were 9.7% and 4.5%. The relative smallness of the German figure is not surprising when one realizes that the German mark was revalued during the 1968-69 period.

One could go on and list experience after experience. One can also from the more limited data notice the precise opposite price effects when a country revalues. While the price effects of exchange rate changes are more distinct using wholesale prices, they are still quite evident using the less volatile consumer prices. Even over long periods of time, the relationship between exchange rate changes and relative rates of inflation remains remarkably close.

On the basis of historical experience in numerous countries, one surely cannot disregard the alternative view of the inflationary consequences of devaluation. In point of fact, it can hardly be coincidental that so much inflation follows directly on the heels of a devaluation in such a large number of episodes. While obviously much more could be done to verify as well as quantify the relationship, both theory and the available empirical data suggest that a devaluation has far more than the trifling inflationary impact which the traditional doctrine suggests.

In sum, I personally feel that the mystery of the current bout of inflation in the United States is readily solvable; it is as much a direct consequence of the dollar's devaluations as any other cause. I would hope that our recent experience with devaluations would make policy officials as well as academics slightly more cautious about panaceas. Looking at the current U.S. experience alone, it would seem that a robust turnaround in the trade balance did not come until the rate of economic growth slowed, but that robust inflation took off as soon as devaluation took place.

—ARTHUR B. LAFFER
University of Chicago

January 1974

Do Devaluations Help Trade?

IN policy as well as academic circles, it is widely believed that changes in exchange rates cause changes in trade balance. Devaluations are believed to lead to improved trade balances, while revaluations are supposed to lead to worsened trade balances. Yet, more than a year after the Smithsonian accord, the U.S. trade balance has shown no sign of improving. According to many people, we need just a little more time for the devaluation to have its effects.

While obviously not definitive, the evidence presented here places doubt on the notion that devaluations bring about improvements in trade balances: the trade balance being one of the major components of the balance of payments, that component thought to be most responsive to exchange rate changes. In addition, the evidence points very strongly to a close and lasting relationship between changes in trade balances and changes in relative rates of growth. The theory of this latter relationship being firmly placed on the well-accepted notion that a country's net demand for foreign goods depends upon its level of income.

The popular theory behind the relationship between exchange rates and trade balances is straightforward. A representative statement of that theory as it pertains to the U.S. might proceed as follows: By raising the dollar price of foreign exchange (devaluation of the dollar), the dollar cost of foreign goods will naturally rise. In a like manner—because the foreign exchange price of the dollar has fallen as a consequence of U.S. devaluation—the foreign currency price of American export goods will now be lower. Americans will buy less of the now higher-priced foreign goods, while at the same time, American export goods should sell better abroad because of the decline in the price foreigners have to pay for them. The end result of a dollar devaluation should be an improvement in the overall U.S. trade balance (U.S. exports minus U.S. imports), though perhaps only after a lag of as much as two years.

Nothing appears to be more at odds with this theory than the current trade balance picture of the U.S. In May-June of 1970, the foreign currency value of the U.S. dollar depreciated by about 6%, vis-a-vis the currency of our major trading partner, Canada. A year later, the dollar depreciated again relative to the Swiss franc, the German mark, the Austrian schilling and the Dutch guilder. Between August of 1971 and the beginning of 1972, the dollar was further devalued versus virtually every major currency.

In sum, during 1970, the dollar depreciated (on a trade weight basis) by nearly 3% relative to our principal industrial trading partners. In 1971, there was a further depreciation of about 6% and during the first three quarters of 1972, the foreign currency value of the dollar depreciated an additional 2%.

While the foreign currency value of the dollar was depreciating, the U.S. trade balance, instead of improving as the theory would predict, was actually going further into deficit. Since the middle of 1970, the U.S. merchandise trade balance has continuously deteriorated, moving from an export surplus of about $3 billion annually to the early 1973 deficit rate of about $6 billion

—an overall deterioration of some $9 billion annually after two and one-half years of continued depreciation of the dollar. Nor can poor price performance in the U.S. be blamed for this deteriorating trend. Compared to most foreign prices, U.S. prices have performed quite reasonably since mid-1970 as well as over the past decade or so.

Although some argue that the failure of the U.S. to improve its trade balance is due to offsetting special circumstances, it should not come as a total surprise to those who have observed other countries' experiences with devaluations or revaluations. Of the major devaluations since 1950, few have been followed by significant improvements in the particular country's trade balance.

For the devaluation experiences of Britain, Spain, Denmark and Austria, the trade balance was as bad, if not worse, three years after devaluation as it was the year prior to devaluation. Of some 14 convertible currency devaluation experiences that I have examined, a full 10 had larger deficits in trade three years after devaluation than they had in the year immediately preceding the year of devaluation.

The revaluation picture is not very different, but there are very few examples, and German mark revaluations account for nearly all of them. The effective number of revaluations that Germany has carried out depends upon how one treats changes in border tax adjustments. But, irrespective of precisely how many times the German mark has been revalued, it would be no mean task to discern a substantial deterioration in the German trade balance. Thus, given at least a casual look at the historical experience of foreign countries, it should not come as a complete surprise that the U.S. trade balance has not turned around since the foreign currency value of the dollar started to decline.

While trade balances may not respond predictably to exchange rate changes, they do appear to be quite closely related to differential growth rates. When a country increases its economic growth rate relative to its trading partners, we often find a deterioration in that country's trade balance. Perhaps the closest of the relationships is to be found between the U.S. and other industrial countries.

The corresponding relationships for Japan, the European Economic Communities and the United Kingdom are also very close. Other factors, including some associated with the special characteristics of individual countries, explain persistent deficits or surpluses in individual nations. But in each case, an increase in the differential between domestic and foreign growth is usually associated with a deterioration in the trade balance.

In the most recent of times perhaps more policy measures than ever have been pushed through in the hope of improving the U.S. trade position. The dollar has been devalued, capital controls and trade restrictions have continued to sprout everywhere, Export-Import bank outlays have grown, voluntary quotas have been placed on a number of commodities, anti-dumping and countervailing duty measures have been threatened, and so on.

In face of it all, the trade balance has proceeded much as usual.

When we consider how rapidly the U.S. has grown recently, it seems reasonable that the growth rate will taper off in the future. The rest of the world, on the other hand, has recently been growing slowly relative to historical norms and should show some resurgence. If foreign growth does rise and U.S. growth slackens, we should expect a noticeable improvement in the U.S. trade balance. This improvement should, in my opinion, be attributed to U.S. growth relative to foreign growth, and not (as it probably will) to the delayed effects of devaluation.

From a theoretical standpoint, the relationship between a country's trade balance and its relative rate of growth is based entirely upon the well-accepted notion that the higher a country's income is, the more that country will import. Thus, as is well documented in virtually all elementary textbooks, net imports depend upon income. Changes in net imports depend, therefore, on changes in income. And changes in net imports, as a share of GNP, depend upon a country's growth rate.

Any one country's imports are necessarily the exports of the rest of the world, and its exports are the rest of the world's imports. Therefore, a country's trade balance surplus is the rest of the world's deficit. Because one country's trade balance surplus is all other countries' deficit, that country's trade balance must likewise depend upon the growth of the rest of the world, as well as its own growth rate. Therefore, based solely on the notion that the level of a country's imports depends on its income, we find that changes in its trade balance (or current account) should depend upon changes in its growth rate relative to the rest of the world.

From a policy standpoint, there are several observations that can be made concerning the balance of trade. (The reader must again be careful to distinguish between the balance of trade and the overall balance of payments.)

First, while no one can say for sure that exchange rate changes do not matter, it appears fair to say that their effects on the trade balance and thereby domestic employment have been greatly exaggerated in policy discussions.

Second, I think the use of the trade balance as a policy indicator distinct from domestic growth has probably been overdone and should be played down. Thus, much of the blame placed on the current administration for poor trade performance should properly be praise for bringing about rapid economic growth.

Third, both official and private pessimism as to the future American trade position also appear to me to have been substantially overstated. While we may not soon again see the surpluses of the late forties, the very recent trade deficits also appear to be somewhat abnormal.

Finally, although no one can ever deny with certainty that trade measures other than exchange rate changes help the trade balance, there is a widely held presumption in policy discussions that these trade measures do matter and matter a lot. This point of view has clearly been given too much weight in trade policy. The trade balance, like many other economic indicators, responds both predictably and in a logical way to the overall economic environment. Using gimmicks to alter the trade balance is to a large extent futile, and perhaps even mischievous.

—ARTHUR B. LAFFER
University of Chicago

February 1973

Bouncing Back

THE comeback of the dollar, still wobbly-kneed but on its feet, promises to lift a bit of the gloom from some big economic problem areas—the stock market, the U.S. economy and the world monetary system.

That's the cautious but surprisingly uniform view of a variety of economists, bankers and dealers in foreign exchange. They see a modest fallout of benefits ahead as they watch the declining price of gold and the slight but steady rise in late summer 1973 in the dollar's long-depressed price (as measured in terms of such currencies as German marks, French francs and British pounds).

One immediate plus: An American in Paris now can get a 50-franc dinner for an outlay of $11.80; as recently as three weeks ago, it would have cost $12.40. (Of course, *last* summer, the dinner would have been only $10.50. C'est la vie.)

An increasing number of analysts in both the U.S. and Europe now expect the dollar to continue to gain strength in foreign-exchange markets for at least six months or so, although not without gyrations. Credit for the turnaround, which follows months of declines, goes to a variety of factors. One is soaring U.S. interest rates, which are beginning to draw in foreign investment. Another is an increasingly favorable outlook for the balance of payments, the flow of money in and out of the nation.

"I think we'll still have ups and downs because markets go mainly on expectations, and these expectations can be reversed. But the trend on the average is up," says Harold Van Cleveland, vice president and economist for First National City Bank. Similarly, Karl Otto Poehl, under secretary in the West German Finance Ministry, said recently he expects the dollar's price to stabilize or possibly continue to gain.

"We have seen the bottom for this year," says Charles R. Stahl, president of Economic News Agency, a Princeton, N.J., advisory firm. "The dollar will be 8% to 10% up (from the low levels of July) by the end of the year," he predicts. This would put it back at the level prevailing before its devaluation in February 1973 and would make the dollar worth about 2.9 marks (against 2.4 now), 4.6 French francs (against 4.24 now) and 3.4 Swiss francs (against 2.9). In the frantic exchange markets of early July 1973, the dollar plummeted to 2.29 marks, 4.22 French francs and 3.05 Swiss francs.

The current predictions of continued dollar firmness don't usually extend to the long term. The dollar's price is affected by so many economic and psychological factors that most analysts say trying to predict for a year or more ahead is futile. But if dollars do indeed strengthen even temporarily—or at least avoid new fainting spells—the effects will still be important.

For example, in the market for shares in U.S. companies, a relatively stable dollar would help heal the wounds of previous dollar devaluations. Two official reductions in the price of the dollar slashed the value of foreigners' investments, even if market prices of their shares went up—episodes that hardly encourage new investment. If confidence can be restored, says William Freund, vice president and economist for the New York

Stock Exchange, foreign buying could again become an important element in the market.

In 1972, net foreign purchases of U.S. equities came to $2.1 billion, not far from the high of $2.3 billion in 1968. In the first three months of 1973, $1.5 billion in foreign investment came pouring in, but it dried up during the next three months. Some analysts now expect it to pick up again, especially through direct acquisitions of U.S. companies by foreign companies.

As for the U.S. economy, a stronger dollar would help to moderate price increases on imported commodities and other goods. The cost of many foreign goods has been soaring, not only because of direct price increases but also because of the declining purchasing power of dollars.

And already, says William Wollman, an economist at Argus Research Corp., improvements in the U.S. balance of payments are bolstering the gross national product—the measure of all goods and services produced by the economy. By one method of measuring trade, net exports were in deficit in 1972 by $4.6 billion, he notes. He forecasts a surplus of $1 billion for 1973. This would be a swing of $5.6 billion for the gross national product, and that, the economist says, "is a lot of scratch."

A strengthening dollar, which can be credited in part to an improving balance of trade, might also have the ironic effect of allowing the U.S. to further restrict exports of commodities that are in short supply, as is already being done with soybeans and some other products. Such restrictions, aimed at reducing price rises in the domestic economy, also reduce revenues from overseas and therefore tend to weaken the dollar in world markets.

But, if the dollar is strengthening for other reasons besides trade, the administration would have some leeway to further curtail foreign sales of critical products. "After all," one private economist says, "we don't want the dollar to get too strong"—a worry he concedes wouldn't have occurred to him a month ago. Cheap dollars, of course, can help U.S. exporters compete in world markets if they are translated into price reductions.

A more stable dollar would also improve the environment for restructuring the international monetary system. During the tedious months of negotiations on this complex chore, foreign financial officials have frequently complained that the chronic weakness of the world's major currency made their task more difficult.

In recent weeks, however, members of the so-called Committee of 20, formed by the International Monetary Fund to overhaul international rules on money management, have said they are making good progress. Their goal is to devise a system for preventing the kind of massive, prolonged payments imbalances that have piled up mountains of dollars overseas and led in recent years to frequent crises in world money markets.

Some solid indications of agreement are already evident. Most notably, the U.S. and other major nations have given one another what amounts to a partial guarantee against possible losses arising from certain rescue operations in exchange markets. According to recent congressional testimony by Paul Volcker, an under secretary of the U.S. Treasury, central bankers have agreed to share losses half-and-half when they arise through use of "swap lines."

Swap lines are short-term credit facilities among central banks through which, for instance, dollars can be exchanged for other currencies up to specified amounts. The maximum for the U.S. was recently increased to a total of $18 billion from the previous $11.7 billion. If the dollar comes under unusual price pressure in terms of, say, marks, the Federal Reserve Bank of

New York gets marks from the German Bundesbank in exchange for dollar credits and sells the marks for dollars on the open market.

Later, the New York Fed must buy marks in the open market and repay the Bundesbank. A change in market exchange rates in the meantime will cost one or the other bank money—a loss that previously was borne entirely by the bank that initiated the swap; in the past, this was almost entirely done by foreign central banks. Under the new accord, the loss will be shared.

This agreement is "getting down to the nitty-gritty of a new monetary system," one economist says. The significance, in his interpretation, is that foreign central banks now have a partial guarantee against exchange losses if the dollar should weaken and that this will make them more willing to hold dollars in their reserves. The agreement is also seen as solid evidence of renewed cooperation among central banks in their avowed determination to foster orderly transactions in foreign-exchange markets.

—CHARLES N. STABLER

August 1973

Reversing the Tide

THE basic barometer of economic conditions between the U.S. and the rest of the world, the balance of payments, is swinging from "stormy" to "change."

It's much too soon to read the switch as heralding fair weather ahead, most analysts caution, but even a slight improvement in this broad measure of money flows in and out of the nation is dramatic. "There are just straws in the wind so far, and each month from now will be very important, but the balance of payments in 1973 could turn out a lot more favorable than anyone anticipated," says Rimmer de Vries, vice president and international economist for Morgan Guaranty Trust Co. of New York.

He and some other analysts describe key balance-of-payments figures now becoming available for the early months of 1973 as downright startling. And they cite two major reasons for the turnaround: booming exports of high-priced farm products, and foreigners' investments in U.S. securities.

Through the 25th of the month, April registered an $845 million balance-of-payments surplus as measured by the broadest gauge, which includes short-term flows of money. (Figures for the so-called basic balance—which excludes short-term flows and which economists call more fundamental—aren't yet available.) Although no one is suggesting that there will be anything close to a surplus in either the broad or the narrower indicators for the year, the recent figures are encouraging the people who watch the statistics closely.

The new optimism that analysts are expressing isn't unreasonable, says a man at the Treasury, who requests anonymity after going out on a limb like that.

No one is yet predicting any specific figures for the deficit in 1973. At this point, all they are saying is that perhaps the worst is over. But that is big news, for the deficit has been widening since the mid-1960s, causing much alarm—and such drastic moves as two devaluations of the dollar. The so-called basic balance—the net of the U.S. trade in goods and services plus long-term capital movements—has gone from a deficit of $1.8 billion in 1965 to $9.2 billion in 1972. Until very recently, it was expected to widen further this year.

The improvement is still too recent and fragile to have had any apparent impact on the value of the dollar against other currencies. Foreign-exchange markets, following the 10% devaluation of the dollar in February 1973 and continuing turbulence in March, were surprisingly calm during April. European currencies have moved upward in value against the dollar in recent days, but only slightly. And the Japanese yen keeps coming under periodic selling pressure, indicating that confidence in the dollar is abuilding.

On the whole, foreign-exchange dealers say, the dollar has been trading quietly at fairly stable prices. But if the balance-of-payments picture is indeed brightening, that means added strength for the dollar in the months ahead.

Balance-of-payments trends have important implications well beyond the foreign-exchange trading desks. When the trends are adverse, as they have been for the U.S. since 1970, they hamper efforts to keep the domestic economy healthy and restrict the nation's international economic activities—stationing troops abroad and aiding developing countries, for example.

In addition, if current trends foreshadow a more robust dollar, foreign investment in the U.S. will be encouraged. This, in turn, could help international money managers cope with what is still the number one problem for the world's monetary system. That is the vast supply of excess dollars in foreign central banks, the so-called "overhang" that makes dollars less desirable as a store of value.

"Commercially, the dollar now is in our favor, but the major problem, excess dollars in foreign central banks, still hasn't been touched," says M. Kathleen Eickhoff, an economist at Townsend-Greenspan.

International analysts cite two key developments as brightening at least the near-term balance-of-payments outlook.

First, U.S. exports of agricultural products have been rising rapidly and carrying much higher price tags in world markets, just as in domestic stores. In March 1973, U.S. agricultural exports hit their sixth consecutive monthly record, a total of $1.4 billion, more than double the export total of March 1972. For the nine months through March 1973, U.S. exports of wheat, soybeans, corn, cotton and other farm products came to $9 billion, up 49% from the year-earlier nine months.

The Department of Agriculture's export marketing service figures that about 40% of the dollar gain in the nine months was accounted for by price increases. A spokesman says the department earlier forecast exports for the fiscal year ending June 30 of $11.1 billion, but $11.8 billion now seems more likely.

Imports have been rising, too, but not nearly as fast as exports. The net agricultural trade surplus for the nine months through March was a record $3.7 billion, more than double the $1.5 billion of a year earlier.

Part of this agricultural sales gain had been anticipated, of course, because of the wheat deal with Russia.
Those grain exports alone are expected to contribute $2
billion during the fiscal year ending June 30. But now
the overall gains for the calendar year are looking much
bigger than had been expected, thanks (if that's the
word) to soaring prices.

The second favorable element is the sizable and
surprising inflow of foreign capital investment. In January, foreigners purchased a net $474 million of U.S.
corporate stock, compared to $269 million a year earlier,
the Federal Reserve Board reports. That wasn't surprising, analysts say, because doubts about the dollar's value
—and therefore the value of shares traded in dollars—
hadn't yet fully materialized.

But what these analysts do find surprising is the
fact that buy orders continued to flow in from abroad
during February. The net purchases came to $438 mil-
lion, despite wild gyrations in the international money
markets and devaluation of the dollar in mid-February.
"Dumbfounding," says one economist.

Moreover, while figures aren't yet available for
March, it's expected that net purchases of shares will
show another gain of around $400 million, despite a
weak stock market and continuing monetary uncertainty. This could make the first three months of 1973 a
record quarter, running totally contrary to what was
anticipated earlier by most international economists.

These two unexpected plus marks for the balance
of payments, agricultural sales and investment inflows,
are combined with the more widely predicted slowdown
in U.S. imports of many products where price is an important consideration to the consumer. "All you have to
do is look at the prices of Japanese cameras and cars or
many other foreign goods, and you can see the dollar
devaluation has had to effect our purchases," says one

economist. "These prices have risen tremendously."

The U.S. trade balance, the net of imports and exports (as contrasted to the broader payments balance), should improve in 1973 for a variety of reasons, economists at the St. Louis Federal Reserve Bank said in a recent report. First, they figure, the rate of economic expansion in the U.S. will slow while the economies of our major trading partners accelerate. This would tend to reduce U.S. imports and increase exports, without considering the effect of price changes.

And second, these economists say, "sufficient time will have elapsed for the dollar devaluation of 1971 (preceding the most recent devaluation by 14 months) to affect demand patterns, leading to a reduction of price-sensitive imports and an increase in price-sensitive exports."

All these factors go into what is termed the "basic balance" in the spectrum of measures used by analysts to report the balance of payments. The basic balance reflects mostly imports and exports and long-term capital flows, leaving out highly volatile short-term flows of "hot money."

On this basis, the U.S. was in deficit by about $9.2 billion last year, almost unchanged from the deficit of 1971. If recent trends continue, some analysts expect the basic balance to begin to show some improvement this year, but they still don't look for massive swings.

"We're not out of the woods yet: we could still have a $9 billion deficit or maybe a little less," says Morgan Guaranty's Mr. de Vries. "But we could be at a real changing point comparable to the British when they devalued sterling in 1967, had a catastrophic year in 1968, saw things begin to change in 1969 and had a tremendous recovery in 1970. On that scale, we could be in 1969."

—CHARLES N. STABLER

May 1973

Made in the USA

FOR years Leesona Corp. of Warwick, R.I., has been competing—largely unsuccessfully—with Japanese manufacturers to sell textile-making machinery to Taiwan.

"We just couldn't compete from the standpoint of prices," says Robert McMurray, vice president and treasurer of Leesona. "Our only selling point was quality, and we were losing sales."

But in December 1973 all that has changed. Now, Mr. McMurray says, Leesona can offer its customers in Taiwan "superior quality at competitive prices." He says that's because the successive devaluations of the dollar and the rise in value of the Japanese yen have combined to eliminate Leesona's competitive disadvantage. The company's exports are up 100% this year, and "last year wasn't so bad either," Mr. McMurray says.

The Leesona case is a striking example of a phenomenon benefiting many U.S. firms these days. The devaluation of the U.S. dollar, by making U.S. goods relatively cheaper in world markets, has sent American exports zooming. As a result, the nation is in its strongest trading position since the mid-1960s. Moreover, analysts generally agree that, even with a fuel crisis developing and with an economic slowdown—or worse—a likely prospect in the months ahead, America's relative foreign-trade position should remain favorable. Foreign customers may buy less, but on the other hand the U.S. probably will import less.

America's improved position is reflected in trade data which show that in the first 10 months of 1973 seasonally adjusted exports exceeded imports by $680.2 million, compared with a huge deficit of $5.23 billion in the first 10 months of 1972. This year's cumulative trade balance didn't pull into the black until September, representing the first time since the first quarter of 1971 that the U.S. showed a trading profit. Encouraged by this trend, Commerce Department officials currently expect the U.S. to show a sizable surplus for all of this year, compared with last year's deficit of $6.35 billion. An official notes that exports are increasing at much more than their normal rate, while there is a "lack of real force" in imports.

Devaluation hasn't been the only reason for the surge in exports. In the first nine months of this year, agricultural exports accounted for about 39% of the total export gain of $14.5 billion. If agricultural exports had remained level with last year, the U.S. trade balance for the first nine months would have been about $5.6 billion in the red instead of just barely breaking even on an unadjusted basis. In addition, strong economic expansion in many parts of the world this year created greater than usual demand in such fields as capital goods—fields in which U.S. products have always been competitively priced.

But in some areas, devaluation has clearly been a decisive factor. Wean United Inc., a Pittsburgh maker of rolling mill and finishing equipment, previously had a hard time competing with Japanese and European steel mill suppliers. But in its five-month period from March through July 1973 the company has booked $110 million of foreign orders, and currently 75% of its backlog is slated for foreign delivery.

Other firms are prospering as well. Du Pont Co., the huge chemical concern, says it expects its exports this year to top $500 million, up 30% from last year. The company attributes much of the sales increase to "significantly lower" postdevaluation prices. To counter the devaluation advantage, a spokesman for Du Pont says, some of its foreign competitors have reduced their prices by narrowing their profit margins. But as a result of this profit squeeze, they aren't aggressively seeking new customers. Meanwhile, Du Pont is rounding up as many buyers as its capacity situation will allow.

In some instances, the devaluation has spurred companies to curtail their European operations. Thiokol Corp., a Bristol, Pa., chemical and manufacturing company, for example, may scrap its European operations this winter. Thiokol, which has plants in this country and abroad for producing snow vehicles for smoothing ski slopes, says the devaluation has made it cheaper to ship its products abroad from its Idaho plant.

So far this year, the biggest export product gainers are in the food, crude minerals (excluding fuels), beverages and tobacco fields—areas that tend to reflect expanding foreign demand rather than just lower prices. In areas where price is an important factor, however, the U.S. has scored much better gains than usual. In the first nine months, exports of capital goods climbed 26%, excluding the automotive area, which registered a 24% gain, while exports of all consumer goods except cars were up 34%.

According to some trade experts, most companies aren't passing along the full devaluation savings to their foreign customers. James A. Newman, vice chairman of Booz, Allen & Hamilton Inc., the Chicago management-consulting firm, estimates that U.S. exporters give their foreign buyers about 50% of the possible reduction, a pricing strategy that partially cushions them against the effect of U.S. price controls.

"To some extent we try to get higher margins overseas to make up for what we can't get here," explains the treasurer of a major Ohio industrial concern. Last year, exports accounted for about 10% of the company's total business, but in 1973 they are running 66% ahead of a year earlier.

On the other hand, Mr. Newman and others feel that domestic shortages have kept exports from expanding at a more rapid clip. Mr. Newman says that most U.S. manufacturing giants prefer to make goods for international sale overseas, while exports are mostly regarded as a good way to dispose of excess domestic output. With American demand currently straining manufacturing capacity, there is considerably less merchandise available for export, he says.

But domestic shortages haven't prevented some companies from registering export sales gains. Hercules Inc., a big chemical concern based in Wilmington, Del., for example, has been hard-pressed to find enough products to export and has cut back its export marketing effort. Even so, the company's exports climbed 15% this year after having remained on a plateau for several years.

Aside from a sales boost, the devaluation has given U.S. companies a psychological lift as well. An official of Morgan Guaranty Trust Co. says that before the devaluation many small American concerns never thought of exporting. Now he says quite a few small firms are going into exporting in a big way. Some of these concerns have increased their output to meet the demands of the export market, and as a result have widened their profit margins through economies of scale.

One such concern is Cranston Print Works Co., a

New York maker of printed fabrics. According to Ray Baron, vice president of sales, the company, its interest piqued by the devaluation benefits, began testing the export market about 12 months ago. Although the company set up a formal export business only last July 1, Mr. Baron says the company already has a "multi-million dollar" export business, which contributes about 3% to total sales.

According to economic forecasters, foreign trade will continue to be one of the few bright spots for the U.S. in an otherwise gloomy economic picture. In a special report issued in response to the energy crisis, Wharton Econometric Forecasting Associates of the University of Pennsylvania says that oil shortages and inflation-fighting measures are expected to slow economic growth in Western Europe and Japan, thus reducing the demand for U.S. goods. But the group says that this reduction should be offset by the forced reduction in U.S. oil imports. "Unemployment should be rising and profit rates falling in 1974," the Wharton group says, but "the net trading balance for the U.S. will continue to be favorable."

—HARRY B. ANDERSON

December 1973

ADDENDUM

Commentary: Reading 30
Developments to June 1974

Since January 1974, when the Japanese yen was devalued (Reading 19) and the French commercial franc was floated apart from the European joint float (Reading 20), important monetary developments have occurred on a number of fronts:

—Late in January, the United States rather unexpectedly ended three controls over capital outflows from the United States: restraints on direct investments abroad by U.S. firms; restraints on bank lending and investment abroad; and a tax on American purchases of foreign securities.

—At the International Monetary Conference in late spring, international bankers and financiers expressed concern about their ability to recycle Arab oil money into investments and the Eurodollar market without assistance of the IMF or similar agencies.

—During the winter and spring, most of the major industrial nations struggled with the economic problems of inflation and large trade and payments deficits. These problems caused the Italian government to collapse in early June and created renewed interest in the use of gold reserves in the monetary system, especially among European nations. The finance ministers of the nine Common Market nations discussed various proposals for the use of gold reserves at their meeting in Luxembourg in June and, in the United States, talk of removing the ban on private ownership of gold increased. These led to an agreement in June by the Group of 10 major industrial nations to allow the use of official gold stocks as security for international loans at a value established by the lender. This permitted a limited use of gold at other than the official price (which was approximately one-fourth of the market price at the time) and represented an important compromise among the nations.

—Perhaps the most critical developments during this period relate to the progress of the IMF's Committee of 20 to propose a restructuring of the floating rate world monetary system. After the Nairobi IMF meeting last September, hope ran high that such a proposal would be ready by July 31, 1974 (Reading 14); however, this hope faded as the oil crisis and inflation developed early in the year (Readings 17 and 18). The Committee of 20 did hold its meeting in Washington in June as Reading 30 explains in detail, but did not come up with a proposal to change the world monetary system away from floating. Instead, the Committee sought agreement on a number of guidelines to make the float more manageable and stable. Thus, for the immediate future, the floating system is the world monetary system and the chairman of the Committee predicted that any restructuring would take a number of years through an evolutionary process, rather than a quick change by agreement. This may indeed be the beginning of a brand new era in international monetary affairs for the world.

Managed Float

FOR nearly two years, international monetary authorities have been hunting a new world money system with the flexibility of a snake, the stability of an elephant and the manageability of a lamb. Now they've concluded there is no such animal and are calling off the hunt.

After stalking the elusive prey from Washington to Nairobi and back, the world's finance ministers and central bankers will meet in Washington again this week, resigned to bagging only small game. They plan to claim as their own the crisis-born creature known as floating money that sprang to life in their midst, and they hope to draw up some rules to help the system evolve over the years, like Darwin's ape, into a more refined species.

Compared to their once-ambitious goals of a complete overhaul of the world monetary system, the accomplishments of this week's meeting of the International Monetary Fund's Committee of 20 are likely to be modest, participants admit. The Committee of 20, which was formed in September 1972 to oversee the revision, will hold its last meeting this week and dissolve.

The deputies of the committee, technical experts who have done most of the spade work for the top-level ministers, plan to meet today and tomorrow, while the committee itself plans a two-day session starting Wednesday.

Monetary authorities originally set a two-year timetable for negotiators to come up with a full blueprint for a new world monetary system. The old monetary order, born in 1944 at a conference in Bretton Woods, N.H., had broken down in a series of exchange-market crises starting in 1971. A main goal of the monetary negotiations has been to devise a "stable but adjustable" system of currency values, not so rigid as the system of government-fixed par values that had collapsed but more stable than the current pattern of "floating" rates, which are determined largely by supply-and-demand forces in exchange markets.

Last September, all nations agreed at the International Monetary Fund's annual meeting in Nairobi, Kenya, to set next July 31 as the deadline for a new agreement. But unforeseen international economic turmoil in the past year has derailed the long-sought overhaul. As the IMF itself delicately explains, "economic vicissitudes have dictated changes in objectives, approach and timing" of the currency-system revision.

According to a key leader in the negotiations, the effort was frustrated by the emergence of double-digit inflation, an explosion in world oil prices that threatens the financial position of many nations, last year's turmoil in foreign currency markets, and a lack of "political will" among nations to compromise their individual positions in the negotiations.

Britain's C. Jeremy Morse, chairman of the deputies of the Committee of 20, listed those problems in a speech in Williamsburg, Va., before the International Monetary Conference, a bankers' association. Clearly disappointed, Mr. Morse indicated that the restructuring he had hoped to complete by now might instead take years to accomplish through "a more evolutionary process."

The rampaging inflation and the oil-price crisis have created such economic and financial uncertainties, Mr. Morse said, that a return to stable par values is impossible for the foreseeable future. He predicted that an evolutionary process will produce a kind of cross-breed between freely floating rates and fixed currency values.

"While present instabilities and uncertainties persist," Mr. Morse said, "we shall have more or less managed floating," in which a government intervenes in currency trading to buy or sell its own currency in an effort to influence its market value. "As and when conditions improve," the IMF official added, "we may arrive at a degree of cooperative management of floating rates" that would almost amount to a system of stable par values. In any case, neither "rigidly fixed" nor "freely floating" rates will prevail in the future, he asserted.

This "managed floating," Mr. Morse said, should be subject to some general guidelines to prevent a nation from deliberately manipulating its exchange rate to the disadvantage of others. U.S. officials and other authorities have said that one of the concrete accomplishments of this week's Committee of 20 meeting is likely to be agreement on such guidelines.

Other concrete interim steps toward monetary revision likely to emerge from this week's sessions, according to Mr. Morse, U.S. officials and other authorities attending the Williamsburg conference, include:

—Establishment of a new valuation for the IMF's form of international money called Special Drawing Rights, or SDRs. Negotiators have decided that in a world of floating currency rates, the value of the SDR should be expressed in terms of the average value of a "basket" of representative currencies, rather than in terms of gold or the U.S. dollar.

—New institutional arrangements, including a successor group to the Committee of 20 within the IMF, to be made up of finance ministers, which would oversee the evolutionary monetary-revision process in years ahead. A second offshoot of the Committee of 20 would be a forum, called a "development council," to focus on problems of less-developed lands. "We are spawning little Committees of 20 at the end of our life," Mr. Morse joked.

—A declaration pledging IMF-member nations to avoid restrictive trade actions, such as imposing quotas or taxes on imports, designed to strengthen their balance-of-payments positions.

—A broad outline sketching out an "agreed vision" of the directions in which the monetary system may evolve in future years—a sort of road map of the distance the negotiations failed to travel.

—JAMES P. GANNON

June 1974

GLOSSARY

AFLOAT: When the exchange rate for a given currency is allowed to drift or move freely beyond values previously established.

BALANCE OF PAYMENTS: A measure of the flow of money into and out of a nation during a given time period. A deficit results when outflows exceed inflows; a surplus when inflows exceed outflows. See 28.*

COMMITTEE OF 20: A committee of the International Monetary Fund consisting of 20 finance ministers representing the 126 member nations. This committee is responsible for negotiating on proposals for monetary reform that are to be acted on at a meeting of the full IMF.

CURRENCY BANDS: A range of values established for a given currency under an agreement. The market value of the currency is allowed to fluctuate within this range before that nation must intervene in the market. Currency bands are usually associated with a fixed rate exchange system.

CURRENCY HEDGING: Buying one currency and selling another for future delivery in order to come

*The numbers following some definitions refer to Readings in which the term is explained in greater detail.

out even on a trade deal that involves payment for goods in the future. See 24.

DEVALUATION: A reduction in the official value of a currency as expressed in terms of another currency; a lowering of the official relative value of a currency.

DIRTY FLOAT: When currencies are floating but governments will intervene in the market to hold currencies within some range acceptable to national goals. The intervention is not required.

EXCHANGE RATE: The value or price of a monetary unit of one currency expressed in terms of another currency. The market exchange rate is established by supply and demand for that currency; the official exchange rate is the result of government action or an agreement among nations.

FIXED RATE SYSTEM: A system of exchange rates where each currency's official value is established relative to the others and the national government is committed to keep the market value for its currency close to the fixed official value.

FLOATING RATE SYSTEM: A system of exchange rates in which the values of the currencies are established by the market forces of supply and demand and are free to change as conditions change.

FORWARD MARKET: A currency market in which currencies are bought and sold for delivery in the future. See 24.

INTERNATIONAL MONETARY FUND: An organization of nations formed after World War II to establish and administer the international monetary system. See Background, Part I.

INTERVENTION: The process by which a government or central bank effects the market rate of exchange of a currency by either buying or selling that currency to increase or decrease its market value.

LINKED FLOAT: See PARTIAL JOINT FLOAT

THE LINK: A proposal that the future allocations of SDRs by the IMF be based on economic need rather than the contribution of that nation to the IMF fund. This proposal emerged at the Nairobi meeting of the IMF in September 1973, primarily supported by less developed nations. See 13.

MARKET RATE: See EXCHANGE RATE

OFFICIAL RATE: See EXCHANGE RATE

PARTIAL JOINT FLOAT: When a group of nations' currencies are linked together through the establishment of related official rates, but allowed to float as a block against other currencies. See 4.

REPEG: To change the official exchange value of a given currency; to revalue or devalue that currency.

REVALUATION: An increase in the official value of a currency as expressed in terms of other currencies; a raising of the official relative value of a currency.

SNAKE: See PARTIAL JOINT FLOAT

SPECIAL DRAWING RIGHTS (SDRs): A kind of fiat money, created by the IMF and allocated among the member nations to be used as a form of reserve asset or exchanged for other currencies. See 15.

TRADE BALANCE: A measure of the flow of exports and imports for a given nation during a time period. A trade deficit results when imports exceed exports, a surplus when exports exceed imports.

TRADE DEFICIT: See TRADE BALANCE

TRADE SURPLUS: See TRADE BALANCE

TWO TIER CURRENCY SYSTEM: This exists when a nation sets an official exchange rate for its currency for certain purposes (i.e. commercial transactions) but allows the currency to float for other purposes (i.e. financial transactions).